How you can m
in the new economy

GIVE IT A

GO

What have you got to lose?

by Sonia Williams

First Published in Australia 2009 by:
Show Mummy the Money
www.showmummythemoney.com.au
www.giveitagowhathaveyougottolose.com.au

Give it a go, what have you got to lose
ISBN 978-0-646-51075-0

658.872
pp.176

ISBN: 978-0-646-51075-0

www.giveitagowhathaveyougottolose.com.au

Contents

Personal Stories

'*Give it a Go*' is dedicated to the three brightest stars who light up my life, Martin my husband and my children, Jer'tarme and Ethan.

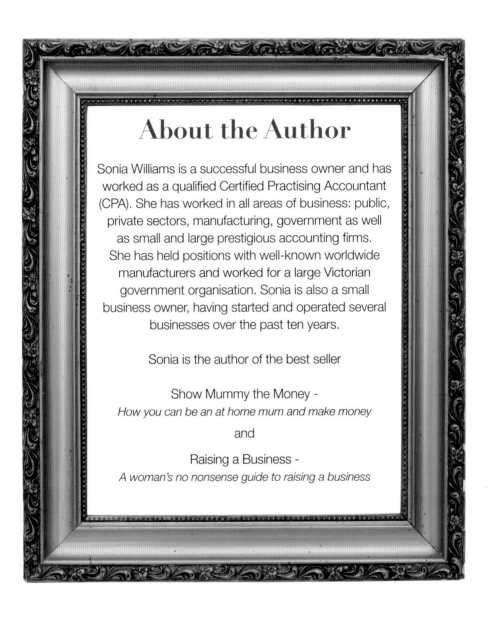

About the Author

Sonia Williams is a successful business owner and has worked as a qualified Certified Practising Accountant (CPA). She has worked in all areas of business: public, private sectors, manufacturing, government as well as small and large prestigious accounting firms. She has held positions with well-known worldwide manufacturers and worked for a large Victorian government organisation. Sonia is also a small business owner, having started and operated several businesses over the past ten years.

Sonia is the author of the best seller

Show Mummy the Money -
How you can be an at home mum and make money

and

Raising a Business -
A woman's no nonsense guide to raising a business

Introduction

Are you searching for a way to supplement your income and eventually escape the rat-race, or do you long to start your own business, but struggle to find the start-up capital? Possibly you yearn for an alternative lifestyle choice, seeking a better work life balance or do you want to discover greater opportunities for social interaction? If this sounds like you ... then you will be extremely happy that you gave this book a go. *Give it a go, what have you got to lose?* is a blueprint that will reveal how you can create wealth, change your lifestyle and achieve what you only ever dreamed of. I will take you on a journey of discovery, revealing the wealth of opportunities offered by the direct selling industry. Over the course of a year I have interviewed hundreds of people operating in the direct selling industry, *Give it a go, what have you got to lose?* holds, the secrets to your success as a distributor in the direct selling industry. This book may very well be the catalyst that changes the direction of your entire life. ... 'Are you ready?'

The origins of this book

Before I take you on this amazing journey of discovery, I want to explain how I myself came to discover the huge opportunities offered by this hidden industry and why I feel compelled to promote and encourage people to consider becoming a distributor in the direct selling industry.

In 2007, I had the pleasure of interviewing the founder of a well-known Direct Selling Organisation (DSO). I was interviewing her for my second book *Raising a Business*. Our fateful meeting was a critical event, as I learned more about my interviewee, I became increasingly curious and highly motivated to undertake further research into the direct selling industry. What I discovered, is there exists a hidden industry that can provide real and viable opportunities, where everyday people can succeed in life, whether it be financially or emotionally.

What this book is about

Give it a go, what have you got to lose?, canvasses all aspects of the direct selling industry, including what it takes to become a successful distributor, what you can personally / financially gain from succeeding in the direct selling industry and the common reasons why some succeed in direct selling while others do not. I will cover why the industry continues to attract misguided criticism, how you can deal with a challenging partner and, most importantly, what you need to consider when deciding whether or not you should give this opportunity a go. If you do decide to 'give it a go' this book will also provide the necessary guidance to help you decide which DSO you should 'give it a go' with.

I have deliberately avoided going into vast depths of detail. Whilst the principles behind each DSO are effectively the same, there will be certain characteristics and aspects of one DSO that differ to another such as the compensation plan, this makes it difficult to go into intricate detail. Instead each chapter will cover the fundamental concepts underlining the direct selling industry, the more important points of what you need to consider and the decision criteria you should employ to further your own independent research.

You will also notice I have not referenced any one particular DSO and the names of those interviewed have been replaced with 'pseudo' names. This was intentional, because the aim of this book is not to favour one

DSO over another or bias your own thoughts and judgements. *Give it a go, what have you got to lose?* is written objectively. The information you will learn from this book is designed to help you form your own opinions and empower you to arrive at your own independent conclusion. *Give it a go, what have you got to lose?* will detail the information you need, to thoroughly evaluate whether the opportunity offered by the direct selling industry is for you or not.

Why did I write this book?

As the author of several business books and a strong advocate of financial independence, I felt compelled to write this book. In contrast to starting your own business from the bottom up, the direct selling industry offers an amazing opportunity for very little capital investment and risk. I have learned the key difference between those starting a business from scratch, and distributors who have a business within the direct selling industry, is that small business owners are in business by themselves, whereas distributors of the direct selling industry are in business for themselves, but not by themselves. The difference is fundamental. Through the course of this book, you shall come to understand and appreciate why it is an important distinction between starting your own business and establishing a business through the direct selling industry.

I have met many budding entrepreneurs, who all encountered one main stumbling block to realising their financial goals 'capital' or lack thereof. For those who wish to own their own business, or have the flexibility to work when they want and for as long as they want, direct selling is the ideal solution. It is the only opportunity where you have so much to gain, and yet so little to risk. Having risked and sometimes lost sums of cash starting my own home based businesses, I felt compelled to let other budding entrepreneurs know there is a much safer, less stressful and most importantly less risky way to start your own business. It lies in direct selling.

Why you should give it a go

In the beginning, like many others, I had little understanding of the potential opportunities offered by the direct selling industry. In fact I knew very little other than the stigma that continues to cloud the industry's reputation. There is good reason why the direct selling industry is often referred to as the 'hidden industry', as many people are completely unaware of the genuine and rewarding opportunities offered by the industry. I had certainly heard of party plan, door-to-door sales and network marketing. Unfortunately though, like many others, I had dismissed the notion that they represented a credible and legitimate opportunity. My research has certainly proven otherwise, as you too will soon come to understand and appreciate.

I hope to reveal and motivate you to consider 'giving it a go'. It is time to get the word out and uncover this hidden industry where thousands of everyday people just like you and I are succeeding in all areas of life. You can create a supplementary source of income or a completely new lifestyle for yourself and your family if you are prepared to 'give it a go'.

For myself the most powerful and compelling reason to encourage people to give the direct selling industry a go, is the endearing fact that this is one opportunity that does not discriminate. It doesn't matter what level of education you have, your work experience, sex, religion and so on. Anyone with the right attitude and determination can be successful.

You owe it to yourself to find out more about this industry and the opportunities it offers. You may well, like myself, be dismissing a real opportunity that could change the entire direction of your life, because your decisions are based on misguided, inaccurate and unfounded information. I believe knowledge; is power, with the right information you can start to make informed and educated decisions. Now is the time to open your mind and consider a new possibility, after all what have you got to lose?

Happy reading !

Common terms

Throughout *Give it a go, what have you got to lose?* I use industry specific terminology, terms probably more common to those who actually work in the industry. To help you better understand these terms and perhaps gain some familiarity before we proceed, I shall provide a brief meaning here. Of course you will gain greater clarification as you progress through the book.

DSAA - Direct Selling Association of Australia
The DSAA is the national trade association and voice of Australia's direct selling industry. With its members, and particularly their commitment to professional standards, the DSAA builds awareness, understanding and credibility for its retail channel with government, the media, consumer bodies and the public. (www.dsaa.asn.au)

DSO - Direct Selling Organisation
A DSO is one of the many businesses who operate in the direct selling industry. A direct selling organisation could model their business on a party plan, network marketing or door-to-door sales structure.

Party plan, network marketing and door-to-door sales
These are all methods of direct selling.

What is
Direct
Selling?

Direct selling describes the sale of consumer goods and services away from a fixed retail location, usually in a home or workplace, by independent salespersons. Starting with the basics, in this chapter I will provide you with a clear understanding of the different types of distribution methods employed by Direct Selling Organisations (DSOs).

S adly many people dismiss the idea of 'direct selling' basing their decision on misinformed and inaccurate information. A proper appreciation of the fundamental basics, will help you to understand and apply the information detailed in the following chapters. So lets start with the three main distribution methods used by DSOs in the direct selling industry. In this chapter I will discuss each method and the advantages and disadvantages of each. There are three types of distribution methods used by DSOs: (generally speaking DSOs follow one method only):

1. **Network marketing**
2. **Party plan**
3. **Door-to-door sales**

It is important to make the distinction between these options as each varies in compensation plans, rewards and method of operation. While having a predominant method, some DSOs will also have elements of other direct selling methods incorporated in their business models. Most common is the multi-level nature of their compensation and reward plans.

1. Network marketing

Network marketing involves building a business based on replication of effort. The distributor has the opportunity to sell product and / or recruit new members into their team by presenting the business opportunity offered by the DSO. According to sources within the direct selling industry, the network marketer generally places a greater emphasis on the recruitment of new distributors, personal consumption of product and building teams, rather than on retailing product to the masses.

The distributor who decides not to build a team, would maintain a single level business and derive sales from just retailing the product. However, this is uncommon. Many who join a network marketing DSO quickly realise, building a team offers greater opportunities to create wealth and additional streams of residual income.

Building a team involves the creation of 'multiple levels' as depicted in Diagram 1. A distributor may start off by recruiting another distributor to replicate what they do. This person becomes the first level. The newly recruited distributor may then decide to recruit a distributor, and in turn this means the original distributor now has two levels. The original distributor will earn a commission from sales made by all distributors recruited beneath them, referred to as the 'down line'. The distributor's business builds through duplication and replication of effort.

As one network marketer from a major nutritional company explained to me, 'Network marketing leverages time'. She went on to explain: 'I was acutely aware I could gain greater leverage, create a residual income if I could create a team of ten other people also prepared to give three hours per week as opposed to presenting to group after group'… 'It's not just about my ability but if everyone in the team can do a little bit, we can all create a worthwhile turnover'. Another network marketer also agreed that, 'Network marketing provides dual opportunities. I can either retail products or introduce other business partners to join me or do both'.

A network marketer has teams, as in Diagram 1. How many teams and levels allowed is entirely up to the discretion of the DSO. You can earn residual income from the sales made by each distributor in your down line. The commission percentage of sales made can vary depending on the depth of the team and the regulations of the DSO with whom you are affiliated. For example, some DSOs will allow you to derive a commission based on 5 per cent of the sales made by members of the fifth level of your structure and 10 per cent commission based on the sales made by members of the first level of your team. When you have developed a structure such as the one depicted below, your role as the distributor expands to one of leader. Your role is also to lead the teams in your down line to inspire them to lead the members within their teams and so on.

The successful network marketers I spoke with recognised that their success is greatly dependent on creating networks and team's, undertaking training, as well as training and motivating their team members to achieve their own goals. They understood that creating levels (teams) gave them width, depth and volume.

The distributors you personally sponsor (first level) provide 'width', and the distributors they recruit at the first level provide 'depth'. It can be difficult to understand this tiered approach, so let's illustrate the structure of network marketing diagrammatically. Please refer to Diagram 1 *Network Marketing*.

Diagram 1. *Network marketing*

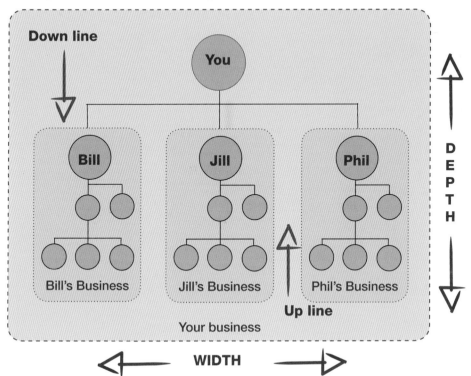

Using the diagram above, Bill, Jill and Phil have their own separate and independent businesses. Because you have introduced Bill, Jill and Phil into the business, they actually form part of your business. This is termed your down line. You earn a commission from the sales made by your down line – Bill, Jill and Phil's sales teams. Bill, Jill and Phil earn commissions from the sales made by those they introduce into the business and that becomes their own down line. You can see from the diagram above that network marketing provides a high level of potential to earn residual income. Note however, that whilst not demonstrated in the above diagram, your business forms part of your sponsor's business (the person who introduced you into the business) and their business is a part of the business of the person who introduced them into the DSO. This is commonly referred to as the 'up line'. Network marketing is a tiered structure: you have the opportunity to build the 'width' of your business by introducing new team members. Alternatively, you can build the 'depth' of your business by motivating the independent business operators you have introduced to continue to motivate the independent business operators they have introduced to introduce new members, and so on. There are several other 'types' of network marketing structures, however for the purposes of this book I shall limit discussion to this basic and most common structure. The beauty of network marketing is that your commissions are derived from not only the retail sales you make but also the sales of the teams within your business whom you are responsible for encouraging, training and motivating. This is commonly known as residual income. The success of your teams bears directly on your own success.

Now that we have covered the structure of network marketing let's get down to the business of what is involved in network marketing. Network marketing involves one-on-one presentations that can be held anywhere from a café to an office and even virtually with new technologies offered by the Internet, such as Skype. During these presentations the network marketer can retail products, offer the business opportunity and / or both.

Network marketing distributors are generally required to purchase a minimum amount of product each month in order to qualify for commissions, incentives and remain an active member of the DSO. Generally the minimum amount required to be purchased each month is the estimated reasonable personal use of a distributor.

If you decide to become a network marketer, the distributor you sign up with will provide you with a customer identification number. All sales made by you will be tracked through this number. Likewise, if you sign up team members to your business, a percentage of the sales made by these people will also be attributed to your unique customer identification number.

DSOs of the network marketing structure have noted their business tends to appeal to couples. Many of the distributors who sign up are couples and / or one partner joins and the other half soon follows. This is because men generally feel more comfortable in a network marketing setting rather than party plan. Network marketing offers the opportunity for partners to create something together.

Network marketers in particular have greatly benefited from the introduction of new technologies. Through Internet technologies such as Skype, the network marketer is able to conveniently and affordably build an international business, all from the comfort of their own home. One-on-one presentations can be virtual. Many DSOs who follow a network marketing structure provide their distributors with many marketing tools, such as the opportunity to build a website to help market their business worldwide. As explained to me by a distributor of a leading nutritional supplement provider, I can be in Australia and training a team member in Italy on how they can grow and increase their business, through which I would be entitled to a share of their sales.

2. Party plan

Party plan, by nature, is a more social form of direct selling. The distributor will make money based on a percentage of the sales they make during the presentation. Distributors are encouraged to maintain their sales by re-servicing the customer base on an ongoing basis. Some of the DSOs who distribute through party plan also provide their distributors with the technology to sell remotely via the Internet. Making it very easy to re service past customers.

However, generally speaking, distribution through party plan involves a host who agrees to hold a party in their home. The host is responsible for inviting and organising family, friends and associates to attend their party. The distributor presents to this group both the opportunity to buy product and host their own party, as well as highlighting the opportunity to join the DSO. The host is rewarded for their participation and the distributor

Give It A Go!

concludes the presentation by taking orders and making bookings with the attendees for future presentations. Distributors derive an income from the sales they make at the party. If the DSO follows a hybrid structure where they can build a team, the distributor has the opportunity to earn a commission from the sales made by any new recruits they sign on.

Generally speaking, with party plan the emphasis is on retailing the product: recruitment of new team members is secondary assuming the DSO allows distributors the opportunity to build their own team.

Party plan offers distinct advantages. The nature of party plan enables distributors to present the product to potential customers who have the opportunity to experience the product for themselves. They can touch, feel and smell the product as they would in any retail store. One DSO of cookware actually trains their distributors to host a cooking demonstration, with the products on offer, cooking a sample dish that everyone can taste. Imagine how much fun you could have cooking up a storm and making money at the same time.

This is another important and worthy feature of the party plan method of distribution. Many of the distributors of party plan report that as a result of presenting with a group they never felt as if they were selling. Instead, they found most presentations resulted in a lot of 'fun', whether it be Champagne with the girls as they viewed a range of lingerie, to the fun and excitement of trying skin care products on an eager audience or experimenting with kitchen and home ware products.

3. Door-to-door sales

Modern direct selling can be traced back to the original door-to-door salesperson. At present several DSOs distribute products by calling on customers and potential customers in their homes. One of the world's largest cosmetic companies distributes its products this way. Essentially, door-to-door selling involves leaving catalogues at homes within designated territories. It is vastly different to other methods of direct selling. The fundamental difference is that both network marketing and party plan are presentation based. Irrespective of whether the distributor is offering a business opportunity or retailing a product, they are presenting face-to-face. Door-to-door selling involves distributors dropping off catalogues where the catalogue does the selling. Strangely the term 'door-to-door sales' is somewhat misleading, since often there is no selling in the strict

sense of the word. Many people misinterpret this method to mean knocking on doors and selling direct to the customer. It is a very important distinction. Since some people may immediately dismiss the idea of joining a door-to-door sales DSO because they fear it involves face-to-face selling, when in reality door-to-door sales requires different skills.

In general, a distributor would leave a catalogue with an order form at the home and call back in three to four days to collect

Give It A Go!

the catalogue and possibly a completed order form. The distributor would subsequently call again to deliver the product. In many cases this would be the only contact between the distributor and the customer. Door-to-door salespersons may be required to purchase the catalogues they deliver. This is entirely dependent on the policy of the DSO. The primary focus of door-to-door sales is on customer service as opposed to arranging parties and demonstrations to present products to groups of potential customers. It should be remembered however that customer service is the common denominator of success in all methods of direct selling.

If you suffer from shyness or would find it difficult to confidently make a presentation to a group, this form of direct selling could well provide you with the opportunity to succeed in the direct selling industry and develop a supplementary income. One director of a new door-to-door sales company said 'selling through catalogues offers a comfortable environment for those who feel they don't have the necessary confidence or skills to sell or present to a group'. The delivery cycle between catalogues varies from three to eight weeks in some cases. The distributor drops off a catalogue, which they return to pick up three to four days later. They will drop off a further catalogue three to eight weeks after that.

Most DSOs utilising the door-to-door sales method provide distributors with defined geographic territories. This allows a degree of stability for both the customer and distributor and provides the distributor with the opportunity to establish and build strong relationships with their customers.

Orders may be obtained from customers outside the allocated geographic area, but distributors are encouraged to operate within their allocated territory. Newer DSOs operating in the door-to-door field are changing the normal methods of operation. One DSO I spoke with explained its new plans which permit distributors the geographic freedom to operate, but provide a level of protection for both the distributor and the customer. This is achieved by guaranteeing that a distributor's customer will remain a customer of that distributor for as long as the distributor remains active in the business.

It is important to note that whilst you don't have to present or demonstrate 'sales skills' in door-to-door sales, you do need to understand this can have its drawbacks. In the door-to-door sales environment you may need to deliver a catalogue several times before a customer places an order. Some distributors unfortunately believe orders will be in abundance once the customer sees the fantastic catalogue they have just delivered. However in reality most people in the absence of face-to-face contact will take their time, familiarise themselves with the products featured in the catalogue, maybe even do a little homework and then, when they feel confident, they will make a purchase. This entire process takes time; you may have to deliver two catalogues before you receive an order. Having said that, similar to network marketing and party plan, once you have built up a customer base, you can work off this base and develop a regular supplementary income.

Give It A Go!

Door-to-door salespersons have the opportunity to build teams, usually within their designated geographic area. Teams are typically restricted to one or two levels.

Not all door-to-door sales DSOs use technology like party plan and network marketing DSOs. Some don't allow distributors to promote customer orders through the Internet. In fact, door-to-door sales DSOs generally have no contact with the end customer. Distributors submit orders, which are filled and sent directly back to the distributor to deliver to the customer. Again this is set to change as more and more door-to-door sales DSOs realise the benefits gained from using technology to bring customers and distributors together.

Because door-to-door sales focuses on the distribution of catalogues, training is less intense. However if you want to create a successful career as a distributor it is highly recommended that you participate in all training provided by door-to-door sales DSOs.

Why is there a difference?

Different products lend themselves to different methods of selling. Skin care products and household products for example, do well in both party plan and network marketing. Fashion products, make-up and jewellery are probably better suited to party plan because of the fun aspect associated with these products. As most women will happily tell you, they enjoy a good make-up party with friends. Whereas other products, such as those related to personal care, weight loss and health care tend to be better suited to network marketing purely because the products provide solutions to more personal, confidential issues. As much as women will readily share tips on the best ways to apply mascara, chances are they are less forthcoming on personal issues related to weight management. Consequently, many people tend to feel more comfortable speaking one-on-one about such problems and related solutions.

How to choose the right

Direct Selling Method

How do you decide whether to become a party planner, a network marketer or a door-to-door salesperson? There is no right or wrong answer since it comes down to a personal choice. You need to consider which opportunity appeals to you the most. The information in this chapter will help you to decide which method is best suited to your character, strengths and personality. In this chapter I shall canvass some of the differences between party plan, network marketing and door-to-door sales, and the personalities each method is best suited too.

P arty plan, without a doubt, is far more social and interactive. You need at the very least to enjoy meeting new people and presenting to a group, many of whom will be strangers. You don't necessarily need to start with a high level of confidence or feel comfortable meeting new people or presenting. However you do need to have the determination and commitment to want to learn how you can overcome any uneasiness. Most new entrants will find their first few presentations confronting. However with training and experience on the job, you will soon find any initial shyness and or lack of confidence disappears. A number of distributors acknowledged with time they were able to over come such hurdles and go on to achieve great success.

Party plan is a little more time-consuming. It can take up to three hours to set up, present, take orders and pack up. The distributors I spoke with found they generally worked evenings and weekends presenting.

The seasoned party plan distributors I spoke with agreed one of the major advantages of presenting to a group of people as apposed to one-on-one is the captive audience through which they are able to easily and readily book future presentations. Presenting to a larger audience, lessens the time spent on promoting and marketing the opportunities you have to offer. One distributor explained 'Because you are presenting to a group of fifteen attendees, chances are there will be at least three attendees, who would be interested in hosting their own presentation'. She added, 'I have found, I am never short of finding new customers to book future presentations, where as if I was presenting one-on-one, not only are my opportunities for product referrals limited to the one person I am presenting to, my ability to book future presentations is also restricted'. This is an important point, when you consider presentation bookings are the life blood of a party plan distributor. Many party plan distributors said that, they found once they got the ball rolling, their presentation bookings gained momentum naturally.

Party plan businesses typically sell skin care, cosmetics, household and other products that are used in every home, every day. Consequently, it is easy to build up a business with loyal customers whom you can regularly service. Success in party plan is about building up a solid and strong customer base, with an emphasis on making repeat sales. Party plan distributors generally focus less on the recruitment of new team members and more on retailing product, having said this building a team, where permitted by the DSO is an important and necessary part of building a successful business.

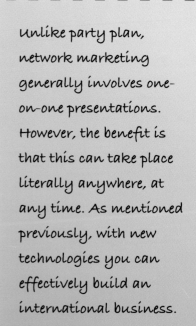

Unlike party plan, network marketing generally involves one-on-one presentations. However, the benefit is that this can take place literally anywhere, at any time. As mentioned previously, with new technologies you can effectively build an international business.

Give It A Go!

Party plan tends to attract more females than males, this is perhaps due to the highly social nature of this method of distribution.

Network marketing relies upon meeting with people one-on-one, whether physically face-to-face or virtual. This form of distribution can help relieve those of the stress felt from presenting to a large crowd of strangers. To be a successful network marketer, you need to continue to either retail product with current customers, grow your network of customers and / or introduce new distributors. As explained by a successful network marketer, 'This can be as easy as striking up a conversation with people you meet in your everyday life'. You need to develop a keen sense of intuition to be able to identify the situations where you could seamlessly introduce your business opportunity or product to a complete stranger.

Network marketing offers a more intimate form of sales, however given your exposure is limited to the person before you, you may have to do a little more to promote and grow your networks. On the plus side, you have the opportunity to use technology to market your business to the world.

Because presentations are generally one-on-one, a network marketing distributor has a greater opportunity to focus purely on satisfying their prospects needs. The captive attention of fewer people for a shorter period of time (usually 45 minutes) provides the distributor with an ideal opportunity to better understand their prospect's needs, explain how their product or business opportunity could successfully satisfy their needs and provide a superior level of customer service.

Network marketing places a greater importance on recruitment of new distributors and less on selling the product. As an executive of the DSAA explained to me, 'Say I was a network marketer and each month I purchase product from the DSO that I represent. I sponsor you into the business with the aim that you will do the same and sponsor someone else. Ultimately, if I can find enough people to do what I do, I'll soon start to derive a residual income. For example, if I sponsor ten people into my business and each orders a standard $100 worth of product each month, I am entitled to receive commission on sales of $1,000. When you consider that commissions could be as high as 20 percent, this means you could earn $200 extra each month for doing nothing more. She went on to say 'Imagine how much more I could earn if each person I sponsored created their own team, the exponential effect of that would be extremely rewarding'.

Network marketing offers the opportunity to leverage by creating teams. Not all party plan or door-to-door sales DSOs will offer this opportunity. As a network marketer you are free to promote and present whenever and wherever. By its nature, party plan is usually restricted to the home although some distributors did say they regularly presented in an office or workplace environment.

Some DSOs require distributors to submit their customers orders, receive, sort and deliver the customers orders. Where as other DSOs, particularly network marketing companies, handle most if not the entire process. These DSOs generally have an established automatic ordering program. Where by the distributor is only responsible for ensuring the customer completes the very first order form.

Such programs are commonly referred to as 'auto ship' and work well

for the product lines which are consumed on a regular basis, for example skin care and nutritional products, household cleaners and so on. In an auto ship system a distributor or customer places an order for selected products for delivery on a regular basis, typically monthly, without the need for a formal order in each period. If a customer places an auto ship order, the distributor who initiated the order will receive a commission on that order every month until the order is cancelled.

Network marketing tends to attract more males than party plan. This is possibly because of the nature of the business. Fewer males feel comfortable hosting a 'party'. If you and your partner are looking to start your own business and / or supplement your income, network marketing presents an ideal opportunity where you both can be involved in building and managing a family business of your own.

Network marketing is ideal for those who have a flair for training and leading. Success in network marketing is largely based on your ability to 'duplicate' your business. This involves learning the systems and processes developed by the DSO as well as training, encouraging and motivating your team members or down line to do likewise.

Door-to-door sales offers the greatest level of flexibility between the three main methods of distribution. Catalogues can be distributed at any given time; if you go for a morning walk you can easily make a drop off. If you prefer to clear your head with an evening walk, you can also drop off catalogues. It is the ideal business for retirees who are still active, or mothers who take a regular afternoon walk. Whereas, with party plan you are generally restricted to evenings and weekends as this is a common time when a group of people can meet. With network marketing you are less restricted as you only need to organise a mutual time to meet with one individual, not necessarily a party of six to ten; obviously this is not quite so easily arranged.

However, having a greater level of flexibility comes at a cost. Door-to-door sales distributors don't have the same potential to achieve the income levels of network marketers and party planners.

This is perhaps because of the limitation placed on the number of levels from which income can be earned. Having said this, door-to-door sales is ideal if you fear the idea of presenting or believe you won't feel comfortable undertaking face-to-face selling.

Whether you elect to become a party planner, network marketer or do door-to-door sales, you may be required to make a small investment. If you decide to join a party plan DSO, you will be required to purchase a 'demonstration kit' that could cost anywhere from $350 upwards. Demonstration kits are often sold to new distributors at or below cost to the DSO. You may also be required to maintain and update your kit as the DSO introduces products and / or seasonal changes. You may be able to

Give It A Go!

cover these costs by satisfying sales targets, and receive bonus 'credits' for the purchase of items for your kit. Network marketers are also required to make an investment. This could be in the form of product for personal consumption. All network marketers I spoke with were required to order a certain amount of product each month for personal consumption, and happily did so to maintain their status as an active distributor with the DSO and share in the compensation plan. Where as door-to-door sales distributors may only be required to pay for marketing materials like catalogues.

All systems of distribution provide equal opportunity to generate repeat sales. Repeat sales is a great way to create residual income. It is important to recognise that it is up to the distributor to seize the opportunity to create repeat sales. It is a matter of tracking and monitoring your customer's activity when they order, how much they order and, most importantly, when they don't order. A successful distributor identifies when it is appropriate to reconnect with their customer to make further sales.

In the end the method of distribution you are best suited to really boils down to what you are comfortable with. Go with your gut feeling and intuition.

How to choose the right direct selling method

Why direct selling provides a source of supplementary Income & much more

The direct selling industry provides distributors with an opportunity to derive an additional or primary source of income. In this chapter I will identify and discuss several strong and compelling reasons why direct selling can offer such wealth building opportunities as well as so much more.

Family and flexibility

Direct selling offers a lifestyle choice. A study commissioned by the Direct Selling Association of New Zealand (1999), entitled *The Hidden Industry,* found that 80 per cent of distributors surveyed felt their lifestyle had improved as a result of their involvement in the direct selling industry, and 83.5 per cent concluded they were more independent.

In todays 'new age' workforce, compensation is simply not enough, workers demand a better quality of life, without compromise. The employee of today understands, it doesn't matter how much money you make, if you never have the opportunity to spend quality time enjoying the fruits of their labour, whether it be with family and or friends. The direct selling industry provides flexibility and work life balance, without sacrifice.

Why direct selling provides a source of supplementary income & much more.

33

Many of the distributors noted, 'I wanted a career where I could be with the kids', with a number of parents pointing out that as their children grew, they found so did their involvement in extracurricular activities such as singing lessons and sports. These parents not only felt they needed an alternative source of income to fund these activities, they also acknowledged they required the flexibility to be able to support and attend such commitments. Some of the more self-sacrificing women I spoke with even stated that they didn't want their partner to have to give up their career so that they could have a career, whilst others acknowledged that they felt guilty staying at home and not contributing to family finances. For these women, the flexibility of the direct selling industry fulfilled their needs on all levels.

The direct selling industry works on the premise that you will be rewarded according to your efforts. Consequently, this industry offers the highest level of flexibility. If you decide to work less, you will be rewarded accordingly. Distributors, particularly mothers and those working part-time jobs, have the opportunity to adjust their input depending on their workloads. The industry also offers members the flexibility to vary what time of the day they work. Parents of small children can opt to work in the evenings or during the day, introducing their product whilst spending quality time with friends in parenting groups, clubs and at other social get-togethers. There are no set hours – unlike traditional employment, you don't have to turn up to work at 9 am and work a solid 8-hour day. In fact, some distributors acknowledged they were able to earn just the right level of extra cash to help make ends meet by working as little as 10 hours per week. The versatility of this industry means you have the chance to work as little or as much as you like depending on your reasons and goals for becoming a distributor.

Give It A Go!

Entrepreneurial aspirations

The direct selling industry is one of the few industries that can offer any and every individual, irrespective of their race, financial status, education level, sex, or religion, an affordable opportunity to start their own business. It is the ultimate equal opportunity solution, representing the purest form of equality through free enterprise. The costs to start your own business from scratch can be horrendous and for many, this alone is the reason that prohibits them from realising their own entrepreneurial goals. Some of those interviewed commented, that they had looked into the idea of joining a franchise however, as they pointed out, this option was still too expensive, highly controlled and very restrictive.

As a distributor of a DSO you are generally only responsible for such costs including:

- purchasing and maintaining your kit if you elected to work in party plan
- a monthly consignment of stock for personal use if you decided to enter network marketing
- catalogues for distribution if you joined a DSO that distributes through door-to-door sales.

Unlike even the smallest business owner, you do not have to worry about the marketing, inventory and or product quality. Being a distributor means you are free from these substantial costs and the cumbersome worries that can plague and stress many business owners.

The direct selling industry offers other benefits compared to owning and operating your own business. Many small business owners find owning their own business becomes more like a job, with the business relying solely on them.

One of the appealing features of direct selling is the low-cost entry; the start-up cost is universally affordable. This is in complete contrast to the independent business opportunities like those offered in franchising, which normally require investments that are beyond the financial means of most of those wanting to run their own business and which generally demand a full-time commitment.

Why direct selling provides a source of supplementary income & much more.

35

Working in the direct selling industry, distributors have an opportunity to create a business they can leverage, which will operate without them being there all of the time and, more importantly, without the business being entirely dependent on them.

Some entrepreneurial mums and dads said they were creating a business they could pass on to their own children. I interviewed one mum from a lingerie company who was slowly passing her business on to her 21-year-old daughter.

Longevity

The direct selling industry offers security and longevity in a world that has long seen the end of the 10 to 20 year working career with one employer. Success in this industry relies solely upon you. There are few encumbering obstacles between the realisation of your own success and security other than your own limiting attitude.

Personal development

The study entitled *The Hidden Industry* found that of the 90,000 distributors and agents involved, 90 per cent felt they had learnt new skills or improved old ones as a result of being involved in direct selling. 93 per cent agreed that their communication skills had improved and 87.5 per cent felt they were more confident.

The personal development and training provided by many DSOs is second to none. Joining a DSO means you have an opportunity to develop yourself in many facets of both your personal and business life. DSOs provide the highest level of training and support to their distributors. In fact, many will happily admit they spend more money on training and supporting their distributors than they do on marketing their business and products.

One of the pleasing features of this industry is the value they place on distributors. In a workforce where the employee is usually the last on the list, the direct selling industry focuses a great deal of attention on their distributors as their first priority.

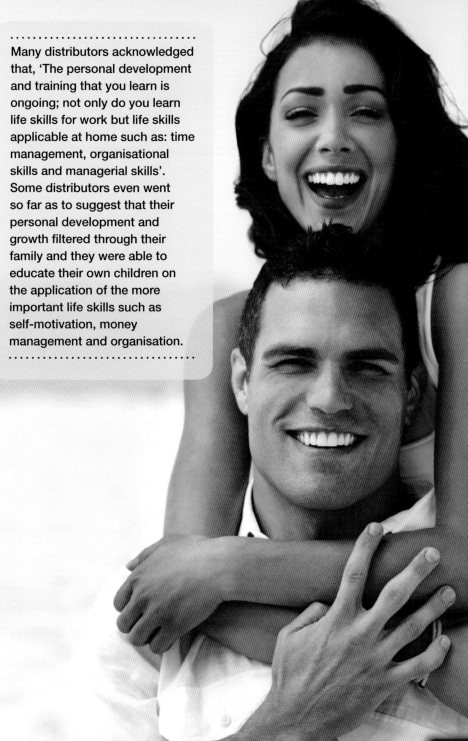

Many distributors acknowledged that, 'The personal development and training that you learn is ongoing; not only do you learn life skills for work but life skills applicable at home such as: time management, organisational skills and managerial skills'. Some distributors even went so far as to suggest that their personal development and growth filtered through their family and they were able to educate their own children on the application of the more important life skills such as self-motivation, money management and organisation.

Why direct selling provides a source of supplementary income & much more.

37

Incentives and rewards

The incentives offered by the direct selling industry are extensive. The industry richly rewards its distributors in a number of ways including overseas trips, cars, even jewellery. Every DSO will have a compensation and reward plan. The rewards are powerful incentives to motivate distributors to achieve set targets. A number of distributors told me that ordinarily they would never have had the chance to indulge in exotic overseas trips like walking the Great Wall of China or bathing in the tropics of Thailand had they not joined the industry. If you are prepared to work hard and achieve set targets you will indeed be rewarded for your efforts. This is perhaps one of the more appealing characteristics of the industry. As many of you will know, traditional employers do not offer such indulgent overseas trips, let alone with hundreds of associates with whom you have the opportunity to create close, life long relationships. In traditional employment, the best an employee can hope for is a decent pay rise, and that's still subject to tax. The rewards provided by the DSOs are a reflection of their commitment to their consultants. I interviewed a number of the owners and directors of a range of global DSOs. Their level of commitment and recognition of the importance their distributors played in the success of their business particularly struck me. Upon reflection of my own working career, the best I had received for my 10-hour days was a 2 per cent pay rise and a token 'thanks'.

IRE

Like to make some notes?

Why direct selling provides a source of supplementary income & much more.

39

Why the
Direct selling industry has certain advantages

The direct selling industry has a number of advantages over and above other industries, online businesses and retail shops. These justifications are incentive enough to consider the opportunity provided by the industry. In this chapter I will detail the distinct advantages offered by the industry, of which you can capitalise upon and succeed in the direct selling industry.

According to the World Federation of Direct Selling Association (www.wfdsa.org), between 2000 and 2006, global sales made by the direct selling industry grew from 82.26 billion (US dollars) to 109 billion (US dollars). Likewise, the global sales force of distributors grew from 38.71 million in 2000 to 61.45 million in 2006. The statistics support the fact that, the direct selling industry continues to enjoy solid growth. Demand for products made and distributed by DSOs has not slowed down even in tough economic times. It is in fact evidence of the industry's strengths and advantages. More and more everyday people are discovering through the direct selling industry they can create a residual income or bring about a significant change of lifestyle.

Mobility

The power of the direct selling industry lies in its mobility: distributors of a DSO can easily place themselves at the forefront of the customer. They have the ability to seek and discover new customers where as a retailer or online store cannot as readily place themselves at their customers doorstep. Distributors don't have to wait for a customer to drop in or a web-surfer to discover their site. Depending on how much you want to gain from the industry, you can be as proactive as you desire. The direct selling industry provides a platform for the 'go-getters' to achieve and excel. Many distributors indicated they were able to easily and quickly grow their businesses because they could effectively source their customers themselves. They were not locked into a particular suburb or location and a few very resourceful distributors even admitted to taking their kit on the road when on holiday.

The power of the presentation

The power of the presentation itself precludes competitors. In a typical shop you will have at least 10 different brands competing against each other. It is harder to sell a product under these circumstances, whereas when a distributor 'presents', they not only have a captive audience but competitors are nowhere to be seen. The distributor does not have to worry about convincing or persuading their audience to buy their product over another competitors – they simply need to explain and demonstrate the benefits of the product.

Give It A Go!

Customer service

Sadly, the notion of 'good customer service' in department stores and retail shops is a distant memory. Long gone are the days when customers were king. Many companies continue to focus on cutting costs through lower wages, consequently it is not uncommon to find you can walk into a retail department store and be sold a $200 saucepan from a teenager who hasn't even left home, let alone learnt how to cook. Customer service is another advantage the direct selling industry has over retail outlets. The distributors understand, appreciate and deliver 'personal service'. They provide expertise and guidance to their customers, whether it is in the application of make-up, the correct fitting of a bra, or guidance on how to expertly furnish your home. Because distributors are properly trained regarding the products they sell, they are able to provide the one-on-one relationship and customer care that is so desperately missing in retail. The power of direct selling, lies in the distributors ability to provide

superior customer service and educate their customers about products and services that will improve their lives and satisfy their needs. Overall, distributors can provide a better experience; they can devote their sole attention to the customer, succinctly answer their customers' questions and provide a hands-on service.

Why the direct selling industry has certain advantages.

Exclusivity

Distributors have exclusivity, whereas a retailer can find they are competing with a number of other retailers in close proximity, all stocking the same product. Where as distributors of the direct selling industry, have exclusivity. The customers of the distributor cannot simply 'shop around' as they won't find the product stocked anywhere else, other than with a distributor from the same DSO. Exclusivity leads to a very high degree of brand loyalty where successful distributors service groups of loyal customers on a regular basis. It is a lot easier to establish and grow a successful business with less competition.

Leverage

The direct selling industry provides aspiring entrepreneurs with leverage; leverage to continue to create and build new relationships. Allow me to explain by way of example. When you visit a department store to purchase a product the cashier or sales assistant will hand you a receipt after money has changed hands. You then take your goods and are on your way. Whilst the department store has a record of the transaction, they unfortunately have no record of you as a person, your contact details, your likes or preferences. This is where direct selling excels above retail outlets. Distributors have the ability to maintain records on all the persons they have dealings with, details that can be used to build future relationships and grow a business in direct selling. As a distributor explained to me, she would maintain the details of all transactions she made. She would even mark these with the comments made by the customer. In one instance, she recalled that a customer had indicated 'they had a preference for the colour orange'. The distributor said that even though it was a year on, she was able to re-establish contact with the customer to alert them to the arrival of an orange-coloured garment in their new season's range. Retail outlets simply do not have the option to recall such personal details, let alone personally contact the customer with an exclusive offer. The opportunity to market to an established customer base is the foundation that ensures a distributor's relationship with his / her customer base continues to grow and grow.

Convenience

A study conducted by the University of Westminster, entitled *Public Perceptions of Direct Selling: An International Perspective*, found 4 out of 5 of the surveyed participants who shopped with a direct seller did so because of the convenience. The fact that the distributor comes to the customer also means there is little chance of facing car park rage. This is an important benefit direct selling has over retail outlets; we are a time-poor society. It is difficult enough to get time to ourselves let alone challenge the growing number of drivers on the road to fight over limited car parking space all just to enable us to access the shops. Retail shopping can in itself be a highly tactical event, whereas presentations are usually held in a host's home, where the environment is warm and friendly as opposed to the hustle and bustle of a sterile shopping centre.

Opportunity

Direct selling provides a real opportunity for those with the ambition to become a small business owner. It can be difficult to compete as a small stand alone business operator out on your own. There is a long list of operating expenses you will be responsible for. There is no disputing it takes a great deal of capital, hard work and stress to compete as a single small business owner. Businesses with economies of scale will always have strength. A distributor of the direct selling industry has the best of both worlds, the opportunity to flourish partnered with a DSO that not only has economies of scale but takes care of the financial burdens faced by many small stand alone business owners.

Why the direct selling industry has certain advantages.

Word of mouth

One of the important advantages direct selling has over retailers is the power of 'word-of-mouth'. Distributors have the ability to provide superior one-on-one customer service, that gets their customers referring their business to friends, family and colleagues. Generally speaking distributors, who represent the DSO, by nature have joined because they simply love and believe in the products they are selling. The passion they hold for the products they are selling underlines the long-lasting relationships they create with their customers. Where as some retailers are unable to create any referrals, because they employ the wrong staff, their shop is not inviting or the salesperson has little interest or knowledge of the product they are selling.

Presentations usually take place in a warm and welcoming environment, like a cafe or hosts home, empowering distributors with the ability to create stronger word of mouth referrals, than many retailers. The distributor is able to effectively communicate with their customer in a more meaningful manner, because the customer is in a comfortable, familiar and friendly environment. Thus creating an experience the customer is willing to talk about.

Distributors tend to meet new customers through referral. Someone they know, maybe a customer, has referred them to a friend, colleague or associate. Because of the mutual referring friend there is a sense of trust between the two parties before they even meet. Similarly in the case of party plan the host invites friends and colleagues who trust the host's choices and recommendations. Even before the distributor arrives for the presentation, they have a group of potential 'warm' customers willing to hear about the benefits of their products and opportunities of on offer.

Reduced overheads

Retail outlets have huge operating expenses such as rent, electricity and rates. These expenses are naturally passed on to the consumer through higher prices, or through the employee in terms of base wage, whereas DSOs have fewer overheads and thus the savings can be passed on to the consumers. In addition, because DSOs have less significant expenses, they are able to reinvest back into their business and this means higher quality products, greater research and, in some cases, better commissions paid to distributors. It also means the DSO has the money to reinvest in the quality training of their distributors.

Give It A Go!

Residual income

Finally, direct selling offers the opportunity to establish a stream of residual income. Few retailers can claim they could do the same. Residual income is money earned without physically having to earn it; it comes as a result of other activities, very similar to the interest you could earn on an investment. The direct selling industry is generous. If you decide to 'sponsor' someone into your team and they make sales, you have the opportunity to be rewarded as well, generally earning a commission from these sales also. In addition, many DSOs have invested in the latest technology has to offer. They provide their distributors with the means that enable their customers to reorder online. The commissions on these sales are awarded to the distributor who introduces the customer and effectively does nothing more for the reorder – it is just residual income. Some distributors claimed that they had the flexibility to choose to work fewer hours for six months of the year, enjoying their residual income whilst taking time out preceding the birth of their child.

Why the direct selling industry has certain advantages.

Like to make some notes?

Dreams do come true

D ebbie always wanted to own her own business but didn't think she had the business smarts to start something and be successful. As a single mum holding down five part-time jobs to achieve a full-time wage and make ends meet, Debbie was far from her dream until she joined the direct selling industry seven years ago.

Approached by a friend already working in the industry, Debbie could see that it offered an opportunity that far outweighed juggling five jobs.

Debbie was motivated to make money just as much as she was to spend more time at home. 'I was working different hours at various times so I could be at home during some of the day', recounts Debbie. Whilst Debbie acknowledges she had great family support, she felt she couldn't be the mum she wanted to be with her current working commitments.

Going into direct selling, Debbie faced the criticism that 'party plan wasn't a real job'. Debbie says she overcame the negativity through realising the opportunity at hand. She recalls, 'I could see the potential, what I could put into it and what I could get out of it'. Unlike those who have exited the industry relatively soon after entry, Debbie says she looked at the opportunity as a business. She credits her success in the industry to this mindset and was determined not to let other opinions faze her.

The direct selling industry offers flexibility and, just as importantly, control. Debbie acknowledges she likes that she can control her hours and the income she was earning. She knew, if she needed more money, she just had to work a bit harder.

Why the direct selling industry has certain advantages.

Debbie also believes that if you have found a product you are truly excited about, your passion will naturally propel you forward. She explains that she found the key to her success is to be proud of what you're doing so that you can confidently talk about it to people you meet in everyday life. This way you won't miss an opportunity to market your business. Debbie contacted friends and asked them to bring along friends who were not in their mutual circle so her network of contacts naturally expanded.

Failure in the industry is an issue. Debbie says that often consultants fail to clearly communicate that they are offering an opportunity rather than selling. She highly recommends changing your terminology. She trains her team to never ask someone to host a party or buy, but rather offer an opportunity to experience a wonderful product. Booking future presentations is more about educating the person about the benefits of hosting a party so they understand that they are not hosting a presentation for you but rather for themselves.

Debbie says you can easily grow your business by bundling products and suggesting or offering complementary products. 'It's not like you are pushing customers into anything – you're offering a suggestion so the customer does not go home with regrets', points out Debbie.

Training is important in the beginning so that consultants are comfortable and give the correct information. Debbie recommends that new consultants take up the training so they give the correct information and ensure the customer receives the right experience. She also recommends consultants accept the ongoing training. 'Direct selling can be lonely; you are running your own business and sometimes this can make you feel like you're on your own'. 'The ongoing training', says Debbie, 'is an excellent opportunity to gain support and motivation'. She admits that consultants find reassurance from ongoing training. Distributors can use this time to swap and relate experiences, which they can learn and draw inspiration from.

When considering representing a DSO, Debbie advises that you consider the compensation plan. How does the DSO enable you, as a distributor, to make money? The DSO Debbie signed on with was a relatively young and progressive company, who has implemented technology that enables Debbie to promote her business and sell from a specially designated web site.

She says the industry has provided her with flexibility and the confidence to know she can achieve. She has the business she always dreamed of with a lifestyle to match. 'If you are prepared to put your heart and soul in, you will reap the rewards' says Debbie.

Why the direct selling industry has certain advantages.

The psychological
rewards gained from
Direct Selling

The psychological rewards offered by the direct selling industry are often overlooked. Many distributors cheered the changes they had personally undergone. All agreed they had experienced not only significant inner personal growth but also growth in their relationships with their partners and family members. The psychological rewards cannot be measured. What price can you put on an increase in confidence and self-belief? In this chapter I will explain and demonstrate the intangible and psychological rewards direct selling could bring to your life.

T he study titled '*The Hidden Industry*' revealed that many of the survey participants believed they have had an opportunity to improve themselves, particularly in the areas of personal confidence, motivation and business skills. 80 per cent of respondents said they believed the industry had had a positive impact on their lives and lifestyles.

Comradeship

The direct selling industry is a community unto itself. The distributors are surprisingly supportive of each other; I was in awe of the comradeship between distributors. One of the appealing features of the direct selling industry is this affinity demonstrated by many distributors. They are not competitive because they are all aware that there are plenty of rewards on offer and they are only too happy to lend an ear to a fellow distributor in need of guidance. Some of the distributors I interviewed detailed various experiences where fellow distributors had stepped in to lend a hand of support. Some distributors had joined the industry solely based on the comradeship offered. The competitive nature of traditional employment often means few colleagues are prepared to support a fellow colleague who might advance as a result of their help. In the direct selling industry it is just the opposite. Distributors are only too happy to help when called upon; the community spirit in the industry is very much alive and well.

Confidence

All the distributors I spoke with told stories of their personal development and growth in self-confidence. One of the surprising lessons I learned whilst researching this book was that many successful distributors actually suffered a lack of confidence when they first entered the industry. It was amazing to hear the confident and enthusiastic person before me had once suffered fits of anxiety at the idea of presenting, let alone meeting a roomful of strangers. Many distributors acknowledged that their personal development and growth didn't happen overnight – they all found they had to push past their fears in order to achieve their goals. Gradually, as they achieved more and more success they began to develop confidence but just as important they realised they had become happier people.

It is necessary to understand that confidence is not something you wake up with; it is not something that the fortunate ones were blessed with from birth. Confidence is similar to a badge of honour: it needs to be earned, not expected. Unfortunately, there are those who enter the direct selling industry assuming they will achieve their life goals through direct selling without necessarily applying themselves. When things don't go to plan some will opt out, directing fault at the industry. Those who knuckle down and push through overcome the obstacles they face. It is these individuals who succeed, personally developing on several levels – particularly those of confidence and self-assurance.

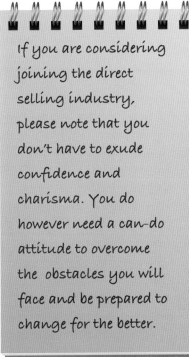

If you are considering joining the direct selling industry, please note that you don't have to exude confidence and charisma. You do however need a can-do attitude to overcome the obstacles you will face and be prepared to change for the better.

The psychological rewards gained from direct selling.

Rewards and satisfaction

The rewards offered by the industry for achieving set targets are unparalleled in mainstream employment. Such rewards are psychologically very powerful; your success is not only rewarded but also celebrated with your colleagues. There are few employers who offer their employees paid overseas trips, jewellery, cars and so forth for achieving set targets, as well as generously remunerating them at the same time. These days it is difficult to get just a pat on the back for a job well done. The direct selling industry is renowned for the rewards and incentives on offer. Some of the rewards offered by DSOs include the opportunity to attend presentations by famous and knowledgeable experts, where ordinarily tickets to such events would cost several thousands of dollars. Many distributors I spoke with said they have been able to travel the world by simply doing a great job. Putting aside the monetary aspect of these rewards, distributors agreed that the achievement of these rewards in itself gave them a strong sense of belief in themselves and engendered a sense of pride and confidence.

Friendship

The creation of long-lasting friendships is one of the more valuable benefits gained from working in the industry. Many distributors acknowledged they had developed very strong bonds with other distributors who, whilst not in the same state, shared the same beliefs, ambitions and dreams. Some distributors would frequently visit the friends they had made interstate.

Personal achievement

There is a greater sense of personal achievement among the distributors in the direct selling industry. As mentioned previously, one by-product of this is a greater level of confidence, however, a sense of personal achievement also brings about a sense of self-worth and self-esteem. Some distributors shared stories of an initial lack of self-belief and worth. Some faced situations where a partner had left the relationship, leaving them to pick up the pieces, whilst others noted their lack of education had a bearing on their own self-esteem. These distributors attributed their achievements in the direct selling industry to helping them develop as better, stronger and more self-assured people. Some distributors pointed out that they felt their personal achievements in the industry positioned them as excellent role models and mentors for their family, friends and especially their children.

Compared to traditional employment, the direct selling industry provides amazing opportunities for personal achievement. In a traditional role, an employee could be competing with up to five other coworkers for the one promotion; in direct selling, distributors are not pitched against each other and successes are not only recognised but also rewarded.

The psychological rewards gained from direct selling.

Social interaction

Surprisingly, many who join the direct selling industry say they have enjoyed the social interaction. The direct selling industry offers a high level of social contact with people from all walks of life. Some of the distributors I spoke with who were mums and wives of husbands who worked a lot, all acknowledged that they thoroughly enjoyed an increase in social activity – almost as if their role as a distributor filled a void. One of the pleasant and attractive characteristics of the direct selling industry is that you are always meeting people who are happy to meet you. When you go to present, it is because someone has agreed to meet with you – you are never faced with the awkward situation of someone who has been made to meet with you. The products and services provided by the DSOs themselves also transcend and promote the industry's social characteristics. There are few people who can honestly say they don't have fun trying on make-up, testing new skin care products or participating in a cookware demonstration.

Ability to grow and develop

In any typical environment such as in our work environment we generally have limited role models from whom we can learn. During my working career I had one direct manager whom I aspired to emulate, however, I had limited access to any other successful role models who worked in the same company. Again, in our personal lives we generally have a limited number of friends and associates whom we can truly turn to for inspiration, understanding and support. Whereas the direct selling industry offers the rare opportunity to access hundreds of inspirational and experienced distributors from whom you can learn. Many of the distributors interviewed for this book explained how far they had personally grown and developed, in part largely because of the influential role played by the successful peers with whom they were aligned.

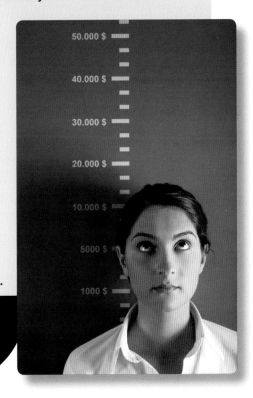

The psychological rewards gained from direct selling.

Words from the wise

J oy has been in the direct selling industry for over 25 years. In the decades she has spent in the industry she has seen many distributors come and go. Joy recalls she initially joined to help pay her car expenses. 'I realised very quickly the direct selling industry would be a great way to go', says Joy. Acknowledging she would rather be the boss than be bossed, Joy stated that this was another strong motivator to join the industry.

Joy says she has both personally experienced and witnessed in others the high level of personal development that comes from being involved in the industry.

Joy has this advice for those considering joining the industry: in order to succeed you must first and foremost be passionate about the product you intend to represent. Joy says for her it was a no-brainer since she has always been interested in cosmetics and skin care. She stresses that you need to be enthusiastic about the products since success in sales boils down to transferring your own belief and conviction in the benefits provided by the products you represent to others.

'You need to appreciate the needs

of your customer', recommends Joy. Empathy for the person you are consulting to is important. As Joy points out, you will find it difficult to build a business in the direct selling industry if you cannot readily relate to your customer. More often than not this means listening to the customer, hearing what they say instead of what you think they are saying. Joy adds that it takes practice and we naturally gravitate to what we believe is best for the customer, not what they truly want.

Throughout Joy's extensive association in the direct selling industry she has often heard the protest from potential recruits, 'I don't know how to sell'. Joy explains that when she coaches new recruits to her team she instructs them 'The customer doesn't want to be sold to, they don't even want to know everything there is to know about the product; the customer simply wants to feel that you believe in the product before they feel confident to purchase'. Changing how you perceive the experience you are to provide your customers is critical to overcoming your fears of selling. 'I find this is a much softer approach when working with new distributors and sits much better than the second-hand car salesman's approach', says Joy.

'To maintain the momentum of your business you must ensure you continue to book future presentations', says Joy. Ideally, you should make two future bookings from each presentation. For new distributors who are reluctant to make an approach for future bookings, Joy recommends that they will feel more comfortable if they approach the question at the beginning of the presentation. Joy suggests her distributors say, 'At the end of the presentation I am going to be asking whether you would like to host a party or are interested in the business opportunity offered by our company'. As Joy explains, stating you will be asking the question up front tends to settle the consultant's nerves and sets the agenda for the presentation. Attendees know they are going to be asked the question so they have ample time to consider their response and the consultant does not feel as though they are putting the attendee on the spot for an answer.

Another barrier faced by new distributors is their reluctance to ask family and friends to host a presentation. Joy has coached many new distributors through this psychological barrier, explaining it is all in the manner in which you put the request. Rather than asking family and friends to buy, says Joy, new distributors should rephrase. 'Explain to friends and family why you have decided to become a consultant. Ask whether they could help you get started by inviting some of their friends to a presentation', suggests Joy. Essentially, you are not asking family

The psychological rewards gained from direct selling.

and friends to spend any money; you are asking them to support you by asking their friends along. As Joy says, it's all about changing the perception of what you are asking for. After all, it is highly unlikely that family and friends will turn down your request for help.

It is important to be comfortable with the team leader you sign on with. Joy makes this important point: your sponsor will coach and mentor you so you can achieve your very best. It is critical to develop a successful working relationship with them. Just as important is your attendance at training and coaching sessions. Joy recommends new recruits take advantage of any training and support provided by the DSO. Training is particularly recommended. Joy says this is a great way to ensure that you are associating with like-minded and motivated persons. 'Often you can bounce and develop ideas as well as inspire each other to succeed', details Joy.

Over her time in the industry Joy has seen many distributors come and go. Joy attributes those who exit quickly to a misguided belief. 'Some join the industry assuming they will reap the rewards without action'.

When choosing a DSO, Joy offers this advice: 'Look at the history of the DSO, how long they have been around and their reputation. You want to be confident they are going to be around for the next five years'. As Joy recalls, 'It was important to me that the company I joined was Australian'. You should also take a close look at the compensation plan. It is important to ensure that if you move to the next level and your circumstances change and require you to take a short break (such as having a baby) that you don't lose your standing with the company. Some DSOs will not allow you to maintain the status you have earned and you can effectively be back where you first started. So it is important to clarify how the status you achieve within a DSO is preserved. Better to know now than later.

'I am a strong advocate for the direct selling industry', concludes Joy. She acknowledges that just as she has seen distributors come and go, she has been blessed to witness distributors join the industry and flourish with a heightened level of self-confidence, awareness and financial independence.

Like to make some notes?

The psychological rewards gained from direct selling.

How to become a Successful distributor

After countless interviews with distributors from all walks of life I am left with little doubt that anyone with the right attitude can become a successful distributor. In this chapter I shall discuss the factors you should consider when deciding whether you would be suited to the role of a distributor. Just as important, I shall also detail what you need to do to become a successful distributor.

O ne of the more appealing characteristics of the direct selling industry is that it is non discriminatory. It doesn't matter what level of schooling you have had, your professional background, race or religion. It all comes down to one question: *'Are you willing to give it a go?'* And this is really a question only you can answer. In my research I spoke with people from various backgrounds – some ex-teachers, others who had left school at 15, some were women with up to four children, but irrespective of their personal circumstances, they had all carved out a successful career for themselves through the direct selling industry.

'The most expensive thing you will ever own is a closed mind'. This was a powerful statement one of the interviewees made to me whilst I was researching this book. When deciding if direct selling is for you or not, be open, try not to readily dismiss opportunities, instead focus your efforts on making informed and educated decisions. I am sure that if you had told some of today's successful distributors when they first started in the industry that they would be enjoying a far more fruitful and fuller lifestyle personally and financially, they probably wouldn't have believed you either.

The big WHY!

The most prevalent factor present in those people who have made a success of direct selling is undoubtedly their crystal clear understanding and appreciation of why they decided to join the industry. The successful distributors understood their own intentions in joining the industry. Before you sign up to any type of direct selling opportunity, I urge you to seriously consider WHY. Your reasons for joining will become a direct reflection of your attitude and determination to succeed. 'You need to have set goals and it doesn't matter how humble', explained one distributor. Before you sign up with a DSO take a moment to ask yourself 'why are you are truly joining'. What is it you want to get from this relationship? And note that I am not just talking dollars. Some of the benefits gained from the industry cannot be quantified with a monetary figure – benefits such as the feeling of recognition, an increase in confidence, self esteem and the strong bonds of friendships that are created among distributors.

One distributor explained to me that when she recruits new distributors to her team she looks at whether the person is 'ready for a change'. Explaining further, 'If someone is looking for change it is because they are unhappy with their present circumstances'. These people generally have the right attitude because they seek a change in their current lifestyle.

Many of the successful distributors I spoke with strongly emphasised the importance of understanding why you have joined. This understanding will help balance out the challenging times you may endure further down the track.

Some distributors recommended creating a visual board that you place in your office or place of work. Cut out pictures of the goals you have for your life and your family's life: is it an overseas trip, to pay off the mortgage, do you dream of achieving a career? Have these readily available so you can reflect upon why you are doing what you're doing, especially in the leaner times.

Some of the distributors noted that those who have entered the industry and failed generally entered with a half-hearted attitude. These distributors see the opportunity as a hobby and fail to take it seriously. Your attitude is a major factor that will determine your level of success.

How to become a successful distributor.

Your passion

Running a very close second to understanding WHY is a passion for the products and the DSO you elect to represent. My research with hundreds of distributors revealed that, each and every one literally loved the product they were selling and the DSO they represented. This was a strong factor contributing to the success of these distributors. You must be passionate about the product you are selling. When you are passionate about a product and what you are doing you are able to sell from the heart.

The reality is that in the world of sales, when a salesperson is genuinely besotted with a product, it is their enthusiasm and zest that customers buy into. How many times have you purchased a product from a salesperson who lacked authenticity or showed signs of disinterest in what they are selling? As consumers, we have a tendency to buy when we truly believe what the salesperson is advocating. In order to be a successful distributor you must truly believe in the benefits provided by the product and the company. People new to the idea of becoming a distributor will generally be 'in fear' of selling. However, you will find that when you feel this strongly you are not giving a big sales pitch or making a hard sell – you are simply the bearer of great news, like a modern day Pied Piper. You need to be proud of the company you represent and this will also reflect on your success. It is very difficult to sell a product if you don't believe in the company behind the product or the product itself.

Give It A Go!

Training

The successful distributors acknowledged the importance of following the training provided. A credible DSO will provide a great deal of training in a multitude of mediums from DVDs, online learning, physical manuals and so on. The training is critical, says one distributor. 'I had to unlearn all I had been taught through my professional career and be open to learning new techniques, systems and procedures'. Another consultant indicated, 'Many people new to direct selling fail because they won't let go of what they know; instead they try to apply their experience to direct selling'. Whilst the training provided by the DSOs is in no way difficult or hard to understand, the fact is that this is a different industry with a different target market of customers so it is important that different methods are employed to achieve results. It is a little like trying to use plain flour when the recipe asks for self-raising flour – you just won't get the same result. It is worth remembering that most DSOs have invested millions to ensure they provide the highest level of quality training, systems and procedures. There is good reason for this: the DSOs understand and recognise the importance of training distributors to be able to succeed in the industry. Some of the distributors said they found the initial training invaluable and pivotal to their future success. If you are considering becoming a distributor, the best thing you can do to ensure your future success is go with an open mind and be receptive to the training and learning.

Even if you are contemplating joining a door-to-door DSO, training will be vital. And whilst there is less emphasis on selling skills, there are well established best practices you should endeavour to learn to maximise your success in maintaining repeat orders and developing a strong and loyal customer base.

How to become a successful distributor.

Are you willing to personally grow?

You need to be willing to personally grow and develop a strong character and this may well mean a shift outside your comfort zone. When you become a distributor you will inevitably have good days and bad days. There is no escaping this – it is life and whether you own your own business or work for someone else, you will still have good and bad days.

In the direct selling industry, just as in any business, you need to weather these days and continue to grow. If you are the type of person who crumbles when the road gets a little bumpy then perhaps you may struggle in this industry. The distributors I spoke with had a great deal of character and confidence, however, they were all happy to admit they are not the same person as when they first started. You need to become resilient to the upsets and disappointments you can experience. Again, it is a clear understanding of why you have joined the industry that will help maintain your resolve. As long as you are willing to personally develop and evolve as a person, you will grow and succeed. If you look at the distributors who have passed through the industry with little success you will find they can list a range of excuses about why they did not succeed. Very few will look within and acknowledge that if they were a little stronger, had a greater level of determination and persistence then perhaps they would have succeeded.

Unfortunately those potentially well suited to direct selling will readily dismiss the opportunity because they see a seasoned distributor present and mistakenly believe they must possess the equivalent characteristics of this person – charisma, empathy and confidence in order to succeed. When in reality, truth be known, it is the experiences this person has endured over time that has made them who they are today.

A number of the distributors involved in my research revealed the DSOs they were affiliated with not only advocated personal growth but they supported the distributors to achieve personal growth. Unlike some of the traditional roles of employment, some DSOs will partially subsidise or pay for the personal development courses of qualifying distributors. Distributors all agreed that the personal growth they have experienced has benefited both their families and their own personal lives.

Managing your time

The more successful distributors had developed excellent time management skills. If you wish to succeed in this industry you must learn to manage your time effectively. Distributors recommend setting working hours and guidelines. More importantly, setting times, dates and managing your time will help guide your own mindset to recognise the business opportunity at hand. Those with poor time management skills generally treat their role as a distributor like a hobby and, consequently, this is reflected in their results. If you want to achieve the greatest level of success you will need to apply yourself by setting clear work times to manage your time so you are effective and productive. This may mean missing out on a few catch-ups with friends or setting time to make important business telephone calls.

Pride in yourself

You need to have pride – not just pride in the products and company you represent – you must have pride in yourself. Pride is reflected in how you dress, act and your overall demeanour. Irrespective of how much you believe in a product, it will be difficult to sell make-up or skin care to a group of women if you don't look the part. Many of the distributors I met were immaculately dressed, not in the latest designer fashions or labels, but well-groomed. They all indicated that this is not attributable to the success they now enjoy but that they have always held their head high at their presentations because they were properly dressed and well-groomed. Irrespective of your social or economic status, we can all have a little pride without breaking the bank. Dress neatly and appropriately, keep your nails clean and trim, make sure your hair is tidy and so on. It is the little things that count.

Socialising

You will need to enjoy meeting new people and building on these relationships. Whilst initially you may not have the necessary skills to build and manage customer relationships, don't fear, you can learn and improve through the training provided by the DSO. However you will need to be enthusiastic and motivated to 'want' to meet new people; being social is a large part of the role of a distributor. There is little point in becoming a distributor if you don't enjoy the social aspects of meeting new people. One distributor commented, 'A healthy dash of personality is required otherwise you will struggle just to interface with customers'.

Patience and consistency

They say patience is a virtue, and it certainly is in the direct selling industry. You need to be patient and persistent – nothing happens overnight and whilst you have the opportunity to create a residual stream of supplementary income, it takes time to build the necessary teams and customer base to create this.

As one director of a door-to-door sales DSO explained to me, you can deliver a catalogue up to three times before you receive an order. It takes time, and without consistency you will miss opportunities to build a strong business. He went on to detail how some distributors had been on the verge of giving up, but he encouraged them to continue doing the 'activity'. Luckily the distributor listened and, as he recalled, they started to receive solid orders by the time they began delivering their fourth cycle of catalogues.

Consistency is the key. If you start to digress and veer off in various directions you will find yourself well and truly off the beaten track. Follow the training provided by the DSO and, if you continue to work at it, with time and patience you will find you reap the rewards.

If you are a person who needs to see big results quickly then the direct selling industry may not satisfy your needs. Having said this, neither would starting a business on your own as each takes time to build and develop, taking into account the margin for lessons to be learnt along the way.

How to become a successful distributor.

A cynic turned success

Alison was not a fan of network marketing. In fact, when her husband informed her of his ambition to enter the direct selling industry, Alison was very much opposed. As Alison recalls: they were recently married, her husband was working full-time and she was working part-time whilst undertaking studies. A friend had introduced her husband to the idea of network marketing. 'I didn't like the idea of network marketing', says Alison. She admits to having a closed mind despite the fact that her husband could see the potential.

Alison need not have feared. Her husband's work colleagues soon set him straight when he ran the idea past them. His work colleagues advised him not to go into network marketing because of its poor reputation: 'Only those at the top of the ladder make the money'. He followed their advice and took the opportunity no further until the night he received a call from one of those vocal work colleagues who had initially deterred him from pursuing his ambition. A respected, trusted and revered colleague, he had undertaken his own investigation and research and found he had given the wrong advice. Realising his mistake he asked Alison and her husband around to further discuss the potential opportunity.

Alison remembers the night. 'I was not very pleasant. My arms were folded and I only went along to ensure my husband didn't jump into something he shouldn't'. Alison says she remembers her husband's excitement when he walked in after their meeting, despite her own reservations that 'it was too hard'. 'My husband was so determined to give it a go that I felt I couldn't possibly ask him to give up his dream', recounts Alison. So she gave him her permission to go ahead albeit with the warning, 'Don't expect me to do anything with the business'.

Alison did, however, use the nutritional supplements and found the product had fantastic benefits for her. In the meantime, Alison received a promotion and began working full-time while continuing to study part-time. However, she became increasingly aware that the higher she climbed the corporate ladder, the more disenchanted she became. 'I finally took time off work to finish my diploma, taking four weeks unpaid leave', says Alison. Over this time Alison began to research the DSO her husband had joined nine months before. She undertook some research and did get a little excited by what she discovered, however, it was not enough to convince her to go ahead. As it turned out, the catalyst that would see Alison join the DSO was a TV program featuring a woman who was taking the products and earning an income. Alison says she could see the potential of the opportunity at hand and gave up work the following week.

'I called my husband's team leader / sponsor and said that I was ready to grow the business and what did I need to do?' One of the main lessons Alison learnt early on was that 'conviction is king'. 'I initially lacked confidence', explains Alison. 'I was shocked at the response of family and friends whom I approached about the

How to become a successful distributor.

opportunity'. She later found the same people who had criticised her had actually tried and failed in network marketing. 'However', notes Alison, 'once I changed my own attitude, I found I spoke and acted with greater determination and people took me seriously'.

Alison warns those entering the industry not to go in with an 'Oh, we'll see attitude', as this will be reflected in the results you will achieve. She explains that it is imperative that you 'understand why you are going in, what you want to achieve and just get on with it'.

She also believes that if you can, get your partner involved, noting that when one partner starts to grow and the other one doesn't, you run the risk of growing apart. The challenge is to ensure that no one is left behind and this can be difficult as you usually find that one person is out building the business and the other partner is at home maintaining the business. It is important to work and grow as a team.

Alison attributes her growth and success in the industry to her willingness to do whatever it takes to succeed. For Alison, becoming a network marketer has allowed her to spend time raising her children. She acknowledges that it provides her with choice and the flexibility to choose. Her husband has since retired from the workforce and they both work on their business together.

Alison offers the following tips:

- Find customers – get out and meet people.
- Verbally brand yourself to let people know what you do.
- Look at the team you are going to join.
- You will be duplicating what they do so it's important to understand their structure and systems.
- Go out and learn, seize the opportunity to undertake continuous learning and personal development.
- You will always grow more on-the-job than by just reading theory.
- Look at the different payment systems.

Give It A Go!

Like to make some notes?

The challenges
You may face

Is direct selling as easy as ABC? No, of course not! Don't enter this industry if you believe you cannot withstand the challenges it offers. Just like anything in life, there are hurdles to get over. If it were easy, everyone would be doing it. In this chapter I will highlight and discuss the challenges you will face and explain how you can overcome these.

Discipline of time management

It can be difficult to be disciplined. By the very nature of the industry, many distributors have home offices. Being productive from home is not as easy as you may think. There are far more distractions that can divert your attention. If you're at home you could find yourself out in the garden when you should be working – the sight of the unkept lawn from your office window is just too much to bear. For the mums out there it might be a case of 'I'll just do the ironing then I won't have to look at the pile of creased clothing'. Irrespective of whether you have your own business or you are a distributor, the challenge is just the same.

You must value your business, it is a good idea to set aside time, mark it in your diary and commit it to your business. Dedication is the key to success. Whilst we can all appreciate that this can be difficult at times, especially if you have a family and / or other pressing commitments, nevertheless it is important to apply yourself if you want to succeed as a distributor.

Work out where you are spending your time: are you wasting time going to the shops each day? If so, you can make time to work on your business as a distributor by organising one big shop once a week. Prepare meals in advance so you are not spending time in the kitchen instead of the home office. Get the help you need to effectively perform your tasks and duties around the house. It may mean you hire someone to mow the lawns or ask your mother-in-law to mind the kids one afternoon a week. Getting help to fulfil personal tasks will free you up to work on your business as a distributor and you will find you are far more productive.

Isolation

Some of the distributors indicated that there is a sense of isolation associated with their role. They went on to explain that it is particularly difficult when you are just starting out as a distributor. Unlike a normal office environment where you could be surrounded by work colleagues and associates willing to support you, the distributor is at home on their own. For some, this can be quite confronting, particularly when they need to make the first few phone calls to generate initial presentations. One distributor told me that in the begining, she would make excuses. 'Oh, they are probably not at work yet'. Forty-five minutes would go by. 'Oh, they are probably just settling into work now. I'll wait a little bit longer. Oh, they are probably at morning tea now. I'll wait a little bit longer' ... then the whole morning had passed along with the opportunity to make contact. She said she knew she was procrastinating and decided that if she was going to be a success she had to be more disciplined with herself.

Give It A Go!

Other distributors agreed working for yourself instead of working for a pay cheque is a challenge. There are many issues that arise from this arrangement that you will need to deal with: namely, once again you need discipline because in the direct selling industry you will get back the equivalent of what you put in. When working for yourself, it can be very easy to put things off, reasoning 'I'll do it later' and then never get around to it. Whereas, if you are working for a pay cheque the chances are you will give 100 per cent because you know your job security and income are directly linked to your performance. Just like a business owner, you need to be proactive and seek out the opportunities where you could present. Again you can see why it is important to understand and continually remind yourself of your goals and reasons for becoming a distributor. In order to stay focused you need to be very clear about what you intend to achieve and by what date.

The challenges you may face.

Training is highly recommended to overcome the periods of isolation. Many distributors acknowledged that attending training sessions and creating support networks with other distributors working for the DSO created the support they needed in challenging times. It is a good idea to create relationships with other distributors from all levels within the industry. Or you can seek a mentor or role model you can confide in – this could be your team leader or someone you meet during a training session. Many DSOs provide technology to facilitate and support the development of distributor networks so distributors can support each other. You can be in one state and still enjoy the motivational and empathetic support of a distributor on the other side of the country or even the world.

Give It A Go!

Disapproving friends and family

Friends and family provide a unique challenge. Don't expect your friends and family to immediately jump on board or be as enthusiastic as you are about your opportunity. Unfortunately, because of the past reputation surrounding the direct selling industry many people, especially family and friends, can be dismissive and complacent about what you are doing. You will find that once you tell friends and family of your ambitions to enter the direct selling industry you will receive a flood of reports and hearsay about how it didn't work for this and that person. You will gain little credit for your endeavours and it can be a challenge believing in yourself when no one else will.

Some distributors suggested it is a good idea to curb your enthusiasm until you have some success. Your success can be the difference between friends and family accepting and embracing your new career path or not.

Friends may believe that because you're at home you're not really working, and they could drop by or ring up for a chat. They don't understand that you have calls to make and business to conduct. How you deal with partners, family and friends is not only difficult, it is important. Because family and friends represent a significant part of our lives I will address this entire subject in the following chapter.

Administration

You need to be organised with your paperwork. It is a good idea to create simple systems to enable you to file and store documentation like receipts or customer records. Some entrants new to direct selling fail to understand the significance of filing, maintaining documentation, creating systems and accurately tracking your sales and costs. Keeping accurate records and tracking customers will help you to identify what you have sold, to whom and when. If you can flick through your filing system with ease you can call your customers a month or two later when you know they are due for a 'top up' and make another sale. In the world of sales you will find a pattern of sales emerge where 20 per cent of customers will buy 80 per cent of product. If you know who the 20 per cent of customers are, you have a better chance of making repeat orders. You need only start with an elementary system and, as you progress in your role as a distributor, this can become more complex.

For some, the administrative side of their business is challenging. You should have a separate bank account for sales as well as a chequebook. This way, you can easily determine the profits you are truly deriving through your role as a distributor. Unfortunately, this is another factor that can contribute to the failure of some distributors. Just like other small business owners, some distributors are guilty of blurring their earnings with the household and personal finances, making it difficult to truly say what they have earned as a distributor. For some, this is the catalyst that sees them exit the industry claiming, 'I never made any money. I worked hard, made sales but never seemed to have very much'. When in reality what you find is that this distributor more than likely pocketed the sales on the way home. Perhaps stopping off at the supermarket to purchase groceries with the cash they had on hand – the proceeds of their sales. Then maybe stopping off to fill up the car, again paying with the cash they had on them at the time. When they eventually get home, they place the loose change in the kid's piggy bank and pop the remaining few dollars on the kitchen bench. Of course, it would seem as though they had earned very little, since the distributor has not only used the money on day-to-day expenses, they have spent it on consumables that, by way of nature, do not provide a physical long-lasting memory.

Not all DSOs require their distributors to directly handle cash. If you are less inclined to manage your cash effectively, then you would be wise to consider a DSO that facilitates the collection of monies owed. Many network marketing DSOs have systems in place to ensure distributors are not responsible for the collection of cash. Initial order forms are submitted to head office, and money is exchanged between head office and the customer. The network marketer simply receives a commission either fortnightly or monthly, deposited directly into their bank account.

However, you won't escape the administrative aspects of business altogether. Building and maintaining customer files is quintessential to the establishment of a customer base that will create a residual and supplementary income.

Irrespective of how boring and challenging administration can be, it is vital to determine and realise your financial success as a distributor. It is also worth remembering that an efficient filing system will also make it very easy come tax time, and you could well reap the benefits of a larger tax refund for your efforts.

Know when to seek help

Some distributors fail to recognise that they need to seek help in order to achieve their full potential. The challenge is recognising when you need help and acting upon this, rather than exiting the industry and 'giving up'.

There may be times when you feel you are lacking in a specific skill set, or perhaps lack confidence, motivation or even struggle to find direction. These feelings are normal; they are also signs that it is time to call in other resources. The seasoned distributors I spoke with said that some distributors will readily exit when faced with challenges rather than seek the help they need to overcome these obstacles. There is help out there and rather than readily 'give up', go to your library, seek out books on personal development, watch motivational DVDs, find a mentor in the industry, or speak to your sponsor. Look into alternative resources that can help you to establish a sense of confidence and conviction and empower yourself to continue. You never know what's over the next hurdle. The Direct Selling Association of Australia is also a great source of valuable information (www.dsaa.asn.au).

A little planning will take you a long way

L isa (a teacher) originally started in the direct selling industry selling educational products. Having stopped work to have the first of her three children, Lisa missed the stimulation of work and decided to join direct selling to re-energise her social life.

She acknowledges she 'dabbled' for six years, not really taking the opportunity seriously until she came across a product sold by another DSO. Lisa, who struggled with sensitive skin, found other skin care products could not compete with what she had discovered, which furthered her interest in what the product had to offer. 'I jumped camps because I was so passionate about what this product did for me and what it could do for others', she recalls.

'After my first meeting with the company I could see that if I did this for six years I could afford to put my children through private school', says Lisa. In the following months, Lisa signed on with the DSO, but this time round Lisa stressed that she had a plan. She credits a great deal of her success in the industry to both planning and commitment. 'I decided I was going to make a go of this so I made a list of all the people I knew'. She then called everyone on the list and told them all about her new venture. She asked friends to bring their friends to presentations and soon established momentum. Lisa says she considered 'bookings' for

The challenges you may face.

presentations like 'lifelines'; without them her business would dry up. Because Lisa set herself goals to have a realistic number of presentations booked her lifelines never ran dry. She willingly admits that it took a lot of tenacity, persistence and consistency to keep her lifelines alive. Lisa explains, 'I had a very clear motivation to succeed. It was either do this or return to work to pay for my children's education. I was consistent and I dedicated a set amount of time every day to build my business. That's not to say you can't dabble and make a little money, but for Lisa she wanted more than just play money.

Lisa says that with hindsight she can see that she did not do very well in her first role as a distributor because she did not have a clear plan or a defined set of goals setting out what she wanted to achieve from her role as a distributor. She advises anyone entering the industry to set realistic goals and have a clear understanding of why have joined the industry.

One of the advantages the direct selling industry has over other commercial ventures is the one-off investment. Lisa explains, 'Being an independent distributor, you only need to make a one-off investment with your sales kit. With most DSOs you can update and renew your kit with bonuses achieved by meeting or exceeding sales targets'. Whereas, as a business or franchise owner, you are continually required to reinvest capital

Give It A Go!

to grow the business. This is one of the most appealing features of the industry if you are entrepreneurially minded.

'It takes a special kind of person to succeed as a distributor', says Lisa, who attributes personality as the main driver of her success. You are effectively your own boss and you need to treat the opportunity as a business. Whilst Lisa admits that anyone can generate a genuine income from the industry, she does make the point that the people who are successful knew why they joined and recognised the motivation that stimulated them to act. Ultimately you can inspire someone, however, motivation is the underlying factor that leads to action. Lisa, who has a team of her own, says she finds helping members of her team to discover their hot button will often result in the recognition of their motivation. She recalls a recent experience with one of her team members who had been in the industry for the same period of time and who struggled to find success. In a succession of one-on-one sessions, Lisa said she coached her to take a journey of self-discovery whereby she realised she wasn't in the industry merely for the money and was able to identify her real motivations. Since then she has shifted gears, having reinforced her reason for doing what she does.

It is important to consider the type of distribution method used by the DSO. Lisa joined a DSO with a hybrid structure. 'I have the luxury of choice. I can personally generate more presentations or I can focus on re-servicing my current customers, or I can focus on building my team', explains Lisa. This is the flexibility of the direct selling industry.

Lisa credits the direct selling industry with giving her family the financial freedom to make different choices and, more importantly, the opportunity to be a stay-at-home mum. She says she has the flexibility to work around her family. Lisa happily admits she has grown personally, going to the top of the marketing plan within four months of joining the DSO. Lisa provides this advice to mums, we can often forget we are capable of more if we are stuck with the notion 'I'm a mum'. We can then obstruct ourselves from achieving our full potential.

The challenges you may face.

How to deal with a negative
Partner, family and / or friends

The support and understanding of your partner, family and friends can be an important determinant in your success as a distributor. In this chapter I will highlight the challenges successful distributors have had to work through with their partner, family and friends. Most importantly I will explain how these triumphant distributors dealt with these challenges and succeeded.

The objections some distributors received from their partners, family and friends were common.

Distributors acknowledged that these included:

- You won't make any money.
- You won't succeed because you have no experience or you lack the education.
- You will spend more money than you will make.
- You're wasting your time.
- Who will take care of the kids and look after the home front?
- This is a scam or a scheme where only those at the top profit.
- You are not a salesperson, so how do you expect to succeed?

The list goes on ...

How to deal with a negative partner, family and / or friends.

91

Before you can develop strategies to overcome some of these common objections, it is important to firstly understand why your partner, family and / or friends are cynical.

Why your partner, family and / or friends maybe cynical?

Whilst researching this book I did hear stories of distributors whose partners were extremely supportive and encouraging. This became the underlying current that enabled and empowered these distributors to achieve a high level of success. Conversely, I also heard stories of partners who failed to support their partner, doing little to acknowledge their attempts to financially improve the family's wellbeing. Initially, I was appalled and felt a deep sense of sadness for these distributors. However, upon reflection I realised that some distributors should be overjoyed by the lack of support. Whilst on the surface it would appear as though their partner cares little for their ambitions and efforts, in reality the opposite was the truth. Some partners care so much for their partner they don't want to see them get hurt, humiliated and / or experience failure. Instead, they opt not to provide the necessary support because they don't want to encourage their partner into a situation that they believe could end badly. It is lovely to think that there are partners who are so protective. If you feel your partner is not as enthusiastic as you are about becoming a distributor, remember, that it may be that this is their way of trying to shield you.

Irrespective of which method of direct selling you decide to pursue, the mere mention of the term 'direct selling' does tend to raise a few suspicious eyebrows. Don't choose one method over another because you believe you will encounter less criticism or opposition – the industry as a whole bears the stigma of misunderstanding and misguided beliefs.

Some distributors revealed that, based on their experience, the lack of support shown by their partner, family and / or friends was a major factor that contributed to the new entrant's quick demise. One distributor said that in the beginning she found the lack of support very challenging. She went on to explain that friends and family, in particular, treated her like a fool even though she was extremely well educated and had developed and sold a successful business in the past. 'I found people outside the direct selling industry didn't trust the process. They would rather assume I had a problem than believe what I was saying. As a distributor, I found it initially challenging. I was made to feel like a fool. I had to first prove myself to friends and family. I found I needed to draw upon a great deal of inner strength to empower and motivate myself, she concluded 'this has made me into the strong and confident person I am today'.

Situations will arise where a compromise of thoughts between two parties will need to be negotiated. You will, as a distributor, encounter your share of negative non-believers, critics and cynics. You might find family and friends can be disheartened with your choice of careers, you may even find close work colleagues shy away from speaking about your new venture. All of this behaviour is OK. Remember, it is different strokes for different folks. After all, if we were all so readily accepting there would be far more charlatans in the world today. On the flip side, the proof is in the pudding. There are many success stories to come from the direct selling industry. It has not only withstood the test of time but it is able to readily boast a long list of real and credible success stories.

How to deal with a negative partner, family and / or friends.

Strategies to overcome the objections

1. Get your partner involved

So how do you successfully deal with any potential negativity? Honestly, there is no answer other than a tough resolve in knowing that you are on the right path for all the right reasons. You must have confidence in yourself first and foremost and again it is a good idea to seek the support of fellow distributors. Don't expect your partner to provide what you need. They are, in all probability, not in a position to understand what you see otherwise they would be doing it themselves. Many of the distributors I spoke with said they sought and received all the support they needed from fellow distributors. Many even noted that it helps to recognise and accept your partner's lack of support is not necessarily a lack of confidence in you personally. Partners by nature are protective, more than likely they are trying to shield you from the chance you might endure challenging times.

There may also be other contributing factors that underlie your partner's lack of support. Some partners actually fear their partners will excel and succeed way beyond themselves. They resent their partner's potential success and literally shut down the opportunity. If your partner feels threatened by your potential success, you need to find out why. Don't be bullied into forgoing your opportunity to succeed. Rather, consider playing down or at least subtly celebrating your successes. Many may question, 'Why should I have to cater for their fears and play down my wins? After all, we are a modern society'. While your wins may be chalked up as one

for the family, if your partner fears your success, they may be facing deeper issues within themselves that need to be addressed. These will certainly be exacerbated if you are outwardly flaunting your success. Seek ways and means to encourage your partner to support

Many distributors who experienced an unsupportive partner said their partners soon changed their tune when the extra money started rolling in each month, allowing them to enjoy more of life's little luxuries. Other distributors said they found that by using a small proportion of their commissions on spoiling their partner, whether it is their favourite magazine or a small box of chocolates, also helped in obtaining their support.

you. You may find that pampering your partner's ego and making sure they feel as though they are successful in their own right will result in a return of the same support. It doesn't take much to reassure an insecure partner; more often than not a few words is all that is needed for them to reciprocate the same support.

2. Get your partner involved

If you are dealing with an unsupportive partner you may find you need to get them involved in what you are doing. This doesn't mean they can join in on your presentations, especially if you are a distributor of lingerie and other intimate apparel. Find out if the DSO has 'partner evenings' where you can take your partner along to meet partners of other successful distributors. They will also hear the benefits and learn about the company you intend to join or have joined. The more you can get your partner involved, the more they will feel a part of your success as you begin to establish your career as a distributor. It is worth remembering partners can be involved in some of the administrative tasks, such as book keeping, ordering, delivering and banking.

How to deal with a negative partner, family and / or friends.

95

If you anticipate that your partner could display some resistance, perhaps you should look more closely at the opportunity provided by network marketing. I spoke with the general manager of a nutritional supplement company whose career covered both network marketing and party plan. She said that in her experience she has found couples tend to be attracted to network marketing because there is a viable role for both partners. She went on to explain that 'presenting the business plan for a network marketing DSO allows both partners the opportunity to participate, along with many other roles'. Based on her own experience she recalls, 'In party plan, all my husband was able to do for me was to empty the car late at night'.

Door-to-door sales also offers a great opportunity for partner participation. If you feel they would not necessarily be open to joining in, then get a little creative. You could disguise the opportunity as a chance to get fit and make a little extra money.

3. Compromise and communicate

It can be incredibly disheartening to be filled with excitement and enthusiasm for an opportunity that could change the course of your family's entire life, only to find your partner does not share the same belief. Don't let this come between you both and, more importantly, don't let their lack of optimism deter you. Instead, agree on a compromise with your partner. You both need to agree to give this opportunity a red-hot go for an appropriate period of time – this is a minimum of at least 6 months. You both need to commit to do whatever it takes, even if it means your partner needs to bathe and bed the children on their own while you attend a presentation. It is important to create the space and means you need to be able to succeed. Some distributors told stories of partners who continually hounded them for results as soon as they started. Their partners claimed they wanted to see the financial rewards for their partner's sacrifice of time, whether it is with them or the family. If you are highly motivated and determined to succeed, you don't need any additional pressure. Furthermore, like any new venture, it takes time to grow. You won't make large sums of money in the first few months: a worthy and credible DSO would never make such an assertion. Be up-front with your partner and explain that you don't expect to make much money in the initial months. It is important to communicate your own understanding of the opportunity so your partner is aware you are under no illusions. Discuss with your partner the kind of support you will need and when, give a time frame and create an expectation so your partner understands you are exploring a new opportunity and this takes time.

How to deal with a negative partner, family and / or friends.

4. Seek other avenues of support

If you feel you are not getting the necessary support at home, consider spending time with those in the industry who are willing to lend an ear. Partners, friends and family are wonderful and play an important role in everyone's life. However, it is best to remember you shouldn't depend on them to be your rock and support for everything you do. This is especially so if you are seeking their support in an area or situation they themselves have little or no understanding of. Get to know the more successful distributors in the company you elect to join, seek out a mentor or role model. For those who join the industry through a member of the DSO, you need only look as far as the person who has sponsored you. Over time, you will find you will develop, grow and become less and less dependent on support.

5. Don't be overbearing

Other distributors said they recognised it was very important not to constantly 'push' their direct selling business onto their partner, family and friends. Rather, they made sure these important people in their life understood how much their business meant to them. Many distributors agreed how you handle the criticisms of direct selling and what you're doing is very important. When facing criticism, try to remain calm, and lessen your defence. You will instinctively feel defensive because you know the opportunity you are embarking upon and the product you represent is not

worthy of such criticism. Some distributors said the best way to handle such situations is not to retaliate. It can be difficult to convince people who are steadfast in their opinion. In most cases, your energy is best spent on more productive matters. Ultimately, at the end of the day you will have the last laugh. As you overcome challenging partners, friends and / or family and begin to experience success, you will find you have made lifelong friendships, joined an association of like-minded people, as well as created a viable revenue stream.

How to deal with a negative partner, family and / or friends.

6. Re-phrase

Some distributors suggested it is a good idea to watch what and how you convey things to your partner. For some distributors when they say they are off to present at a 'party', the word 'party' conjures up an entirely different image for the partner who may be relegated to home duties and looking after the kids. The words 'party plan' are synonymous with the industry, however sadly the word 'party' can raise a red flag for some partners. Instead try using alternative phrases such as 'going to work and / or a demonstration'. The term 'work or demonstration' creates a far better perception of why you are sacrificing time away from your partner and family. Again, it is important to engage your partner so they understand the value of what you do and how it will impact them.

Sadly, many people succumb to the demands of their partners. They miss out on a real opportunity and perhaps spend their lives wondering 'what if?' Mothers of small children are particularly susceptible to their partner's demands and many mothers will begin to experience feelings of guilt if they perceive their partner believes they are not adequately looking after the family. Don't allow a partner to be your barrier. Consider your partner, their needs and their personality and try to negotiate an arrangement that suits you both. An unsupportive partner should never be an excuse to stop doing something you know you will enjoy, are keen to pursue and which will be of benefit to the family. Use your partner's lack of support as a source of motivation; you need to succeed in direct selling in order to prove yourself to them.

Give It A Go!

Like to make some notes?

How to deal with a negative partner, family and / or friends.

101

Spoilt for choice:
How to pick the right Direct Selling Organisation

At this point you're probably very interested in exploring the opportunities offered by the direct selling industry. The next point of call is selecting the right DSO for you. In this chapter I will address the important factors you should take into consideration when evaluating and selecting a DSO to represent.

For many the choice is simple because they are in love with the product. Besides a deep passion for the benefits of the product you need to take into account a number of other considerations to ensure you select the DSO best suited to you. The following list is in no particular order:

Spoilt for choice: How to pick the right Direct Selling Organisation.

103

Satisfying your financial goals

Ask yourself what you want to financially gain from the opportunity? How much do you want to earn? Is it $500 or $1,000 dollars a month? You need to identify how much money you ideally want to make and then work out whether you could earn this or not. To be able to accurately answer this question you will need to understand and appreciate a number of financial considerations associated with the opportunity. These include:

● What will your sales kit cost? Will you need to replenish your sales kit i.e. because of seasonal changes or changes to the product range and, if so, how often? In addition, what bonuses does the DSO offer to help you overcome the cost of maintaining your kit? Some DSOs will subsidise the cost of maintaining a sales kit for distributors who achieve set sales targets. Others may provide incentives to qualify for kit upgrades. New consultants can be eligible for free product if they achieve a designated number of presentations within a set period of time from their commencement. The cost of your kit is a double edged sword; you need to maintain it to make sales, however, the costs of regularly upgrading your kit may impact the profits you earn. Note: It is important to ascertain whether you need to purchase your kit or rent the kit. If you rent the kit you will have to hand it back at the end. This is also a factor you will need to take into account because effectively, if you don't own the kit you will pay a fee with no asset at the end.

- If you decide to join a network marketing DSO, you won't need to purchase a kit – you will have to commit to purchasing a set amount of product for personal consumption.

- If you are joining a door-to-door sales DSO, you may have to pay for catalogues and so you need to investigate whether you will be compensated with a better commission rate.

- If you join a party plan or network marketing DSO you may be required to pay for your own marketing material such as catalogues and brochures. The cost of marketing materials will also impact your ability to generate a profit.

- Some DSOs require their distributors to pay for the gifts supplied to the hostess for hosting the party. It is important to find out the average cost of these gifts and how much they will impact your profits.

- Time is money – it is just as important to identify what hourly rate you could expect to receive between various DSOs. For party plan DSOs base your analysis on an average presentation time of 3 hours: find out the average amount of sales made during a 3-hour presentation and divide by 3 hours. What is the average hourly rate? The same formulation applies to network marketing; base your time on a presentation lasting 45 minutes. Given the level of work required, do you believe this is commensurate with the effort employed? Please note that if you need to pick up, pack and deliver your orders then you will need to factor in this time as well.

- Do you need to pay for your own training? If you are required to pay for initial training, be wary. Most DSOs will require you to purchase the sales kit and / or catalogues during your initial introduction. However, proceed with great caution if you are required to pay for training, particularly if payment for training is required before you have purchased the sales kit.

Spoilt for choice: How to pick the right Direct Selling Organisation.

I strongly encourage and recommend you seek a thorough understanding of the mechanics of the remuneration plan. With a greater appreciation of the remuneration structure you can use the features of the plan to build a strong and viable stream of residual income and maximise your opportunity to succeed.

Philanthropy

Look at the history of the DSO. Are they genuinely interested in the wellbeing of their distributors? A good measure is the depth of training and support freely provided to distributors. You could also look at the charities and causes the company supports. Many DSOs support organisations, charities and associations indirectly related to their product, their mission or their philosophy. It is testament to a company who is prepared to readily give back to their community.

The product

Examine the product distributed by the DSO; is it a quality product? Will it result in repeat sales? A product that is well made, used in every home on a regular basis and represents value for money will always result in repeat sales. Repeat sales are an integral part of any distributor's business. An easy way to make money and grow your business is through repeat sales. When a customer has experienced a product they've enjoyed, they begin to trust the brand and are happy to simply reorder without the necessity of meeting their distributor. Repeat sales can save a distributor a minimum of three hours, time that could be well spent appealing to new customers.

Hence it is important to ensure the product you wish to represent will readily result in repeat sales.

Just as importantly, what is the product's point of difference? It is very difficult to sell a product that lacks a unique point of difference since the customer can effectively purchase similar products elsewhere. A product has a unique point of difference, when the products of competing businesses are not perfect substitutes. For example, a point of difference may reside in the level of research undertaken in the manufacture and design of the product, or the materials used to manufacture the product.

Is the product appropriately priced? If it is far more expensive than other products available to the consumer you will have a harder time convincing the consumer of its benefits. Bear in mind that your job as a distributor is to provide the customer with enough motivation and information to swap brands. Customers are brand loyal: the product range of the DSO you represent should be competitively priced. If you're not sure, do some research and see what the market is prepared to pay. This will give you an indication as to whether the price point will be an issue or not.

If you are trying to decide between door-to-door DSOs, product quality and price points are of particular importance in your selection criteria. As a door-to-door sales distributor you will be relying on the strength of the product, brand and price point to strike a chord with a potential customer. It is very important to assess whether the product is worthy of standing on its own merits in the absence of a salesperson to highlight its unique selling points.

Spoilt for choice: How to pick the right Direct Selling Organisation.

107

Systems

It is very important to review the systems implemented by the DSO. This point is probably more applicable to network marketers since the success of network marketers is, in part, based on the distributor's ability to replicate the DSOs business model by following the systems they have created. 'Duplication of effort is the key' you need to be happy and confident that you will enjoy duplicating the same effort demonstrated by your sponsor. If you are not happy with the DSOs business model, then you will probably struggle to successfully duplicate the systems and procedures required by the DSO to profit.

The level of customer support

What level of customer support does the DSO provide? Some DSOs will take all returns and handle the associated paperwork. It is important to ascertain who takes care of the returns and faulty products: the last thing you need, as a distributor, is to be administratively captive. You want to be free of distractions from the core of your business. If the distributors are responsible for returns and faulty products, identify the process and how much work is involved, including on average how often this could occur.

Give It A Go!

Reputation

What sort of reputation does the DSO have in the industry? Some distributors who have joined a brand new DSO have said that they actually found this a plus. The market was not flooded with their products and they had a blank canvas, so to speak. Having said this, joining a new or recent entrant into the direct selling industry can have disadvantages. It takes time to build a reputation and word-of-mouth, well-established DSOs already have a distinguished and recognisable brand name, thus making it easier to sell products.

However, a word of caution! Be careful whose advice you take on board. As discussed in a previous chapter, those who have had a negative experience in direct selling may incorrectly advise you based on their own experiences. To appreciate the advice given by friends and families you should also recognise the circumstances that gave rise to the experience.

> Do your own research, what is the story behind the DSO? Most DSOs have an interesting tale to tell, about how they started and why they started. This can be an interesting reflection of the integrity of the DSO.

Spoilt for choice: How to pick the right Direct Selling Organisation.

109

Technology

Look at how the DSO incorporates the technology available to them. Does the DSO provide distributors with access to online ordering? The Internet has provided a number of opportunities for the small business owner and, likewise, some DSOs have also seized upon the latest available technology to assist their distributors in achieving their goals. There is a growing number of DSOs offering their distributors their own 'online shopping cart'. A distributor can confidently pass on a web address that allows a customer to login and conveniently reorder. The distributor is awarded the commissions for these sales. DSOs who have implemented this level of technology empower a distributor to continue a relationship with their customers with very little effort.

Does the DSO allow their distributors to place their orders online? Prior to the introduction of the Internet, orders were usually paper-based, with multiple 'carbon' copies. Some DSOs now provide their distributors with an opportunity to login and conveniently enter their orders so that instead of shuffling paperwork, losing orders and wasting paper, the distributor can login after holding a presentation and electronically enter their orders.

Some DSOs provide their distributors with access to reports that detail the sales made by their customers over the course of a specific period.

Check whether the DSO provides this vital information. You can use such reports to check on which customers are ordering and those who are not. This information is important since it provides the details of who you can call upon to see why they have not placed an order – some customers just need a reminder.

Give It A Go!

Your responsibilities

Find out who is responsible for picking up and packing the orders. Here is where there is a distinct difference between party plan, door-to-door sales distributors and network marketers. Network marketers simply ensure the customer completes the first initial form, which usually places the customer on an auto-shipment program. In this situation the network marketer is not responsible for the delivery of product, returns or even reorders. The customer is automatically billed for direct monthly deliveries of product until the customer opts out. The main responsibility of the network marketer is twofold: to maintain the relationship with the customer, introducing products that could be of further assistance to the customer, and / or continuing to motivate, empower and encourage their team members to excel and achieve sales targets.

Whereas the responsibilities of those in party plan will vary from DSO to DSO. Some DSOs of party plan will pick, pack and send the order directly to the customer, whilst others like those in door-to-door sales will send the distributor a box full of their current orders. It is then the responsibility of the distributor to sort the contents of the box according to their customers' orders and physically deliver the orders. It is important to take this into consideration when assessing a DSO. If you have to pick and pack you are spending time working in the business not on the business. Some distributors feel their time is better spent focusing on booking future presentations and growing their networks.

Having said this, other distributors like those in door-to-door sales suggested that picking, packing and delivering their orders provided them with the opportunity to maintain contact with their customers, generate repeat sales and build stronger customer relationships.

Spoilt for choice: How to pick the right Direct Selling Organisation.

Support and training

What level of support and training is provided to the distributors? Investigate the level of training and support provided by the DSO. Don't limit your research to merely training. What level of assistance do they provide to help distributors personally grow? A number of DSOs provide heavily subsidised courses for qualifying distributors.

How is the training delivered? Do they provide a range of training from hands on, visual, reading material of all different types to suit different learning styles? For some, it may be difficult to physically attend every training session due to family commitments. How does the DSO accommodate such situations? Many DSOs utilise the latest technology. They have downloadable video training and tutorials and provide DVDs, whilst others have video conferencing. Taking into account your own personal circumstances, lifestyle, schedule and commitments, how would you best undertake training? Is there a mutuality with the DSO you may be considering?

Besides training, what level of support is provided by the DSO? Do you have a team leader whom you can turn to for advice, guidance or a friendly ear? All distributors interviewed said they faced difficult and challenging times but, nonetheless, they were grateful they had a support person, a team leader or sponsor they could turn to for support.

Evaluate the support structure provided by the DSO; will you receive the level of support you believe you will need to succeed? One of the real strengths of a multi-level system is that you can always have access to advice from your up line leaders.

Restrictions

Some DSOs require their distributors to host a minimum number of presentations over a set period; others may require you to make a minimum level of sales or order a minimum amount of product. It is important to understand your obligations under the distribution arrangement with the DSO. If you need to undertake a minimum number of presentations, for example, you may find the arrangement with this particular DSO is less flexible than with others. You may be required to order a certain amount of product each month. One distributor noted that if your relationship with a DSO is dependent on the number of parties you have to hold per month, it becomes someone else's business and changes from the company providing a business you can run for yourself, to simply working for someone else. Many distributors agreed that one of the appealing features of the direct selling industry is the flexibility. A minimum restriction on the number of presentations you must hold will certainly reduce your level of flexibility.

Some DSOs will require distributors to reach certain sales targets each month to qualify as an active distributor and receive bonus payments. It is important that you are comfortable with the DSOs targets. If you feel they could cause you undue pressure then you would be wise to seek an alternative DSO.

Some DSOs allow their distributors to grow their business through sponsoring distributors and building teams. You will need to understand and appreciate the number of levels you can effectively build your team. Some DSOs limit their distributors to a certain number of levels the less restrictions there are on the number of levels the greater opportunity you have to build your business.

Finally, some DSOs will require you to order a minimum amount of product. This is typically the case with network marketers. To maintain an active status you may be required to order a minimum amount of product for personal consumption. It is a good idea to work out how much and whether you will be capable of personally consuming this amount.

Spoilt for choice: How to pick the right Direct Selling Organisation.

113

The distributors

Try to get a feel for and understanding of the persons attracted to the specific DSO you are interested in joining. It is important that you feel you will 'fit in'. Direct selling is an extremely social industry – not only do you get to constantly meet new people, you will find that because of the number of social events and training available to distributors, you will create long-lasting friendships with other distributors. Would you be comfortable creating and maintaining friendships with potential fellow distributors? As you begin to achieve success you will find you become eligible for rewards and some rewards involve socialising with other distributors at conventions, conferences or holidays away. Since you will be socialising with fellow distributors, look at the cross-section of people attracted to the particular distributor and ask yourself whether you feel you could 'easily socialise' with this group. Look at the values of the DSO and ensure that its values are a reflection of your own. If the DSOs values appeal, the chances are you will feel comfortable with fellow distributors. Pick a DSO with a style and culture that suits you. You are not obliged to go with the first DSO you meet.

Marketing

What sort of marketing strategy does the DSO employ? It is important to research how the DSO markets and promotes their product range. It will be harder to distribute a product few people are aware of because the DSO does little to promote brand and product awareness. It is far easier to get behind a product where there is general public brand awareness. Look at the type of marketing strategy implemented by the DSO. Is it effective and does it appeal to the target market? A DSO who believes in their product will have a range of marketing tools to appeal to a number of target markets.

You should also look into what marketing and advertising you can personally undertake to promote and market yourself. Some DSOs will allow their distributors to advertise, create their own web site and e-market to customers. Whereas others place restrictions on how and where their logos and corporate branding is used. If you are unable to promote yourself, you may find you are limited in the ways and means you can appeal to new customers.

Marketing is of particular importance to door-to-door sales distributors. Look for a DSO that actively markets their business and has a great looking catalogue. Without direct contact provided by a salesperson, it will be even harder to earn a sale if the potential customer has no idea of the DSO you represent. Similarly it is harder to sell a product from an unattractive catalogue. An ideal door-to-door sales DSO needs to be well known and have a positive reputation.

Spoilt for choice: How to pick the right Direct Selling Organisation.

Should a DSO be a member of the DSAA?

The Direct Selling Association of Australia is an association of DSOs. It has established practice standards which its members must follow; this encourages a level of consistency among its members particularly with respect to protecting the consumers of their products. The DSAA promotes and protects the ideals and opportunities of the direct selling industry.

Having said this it is not mandatory for a DSO to be affiliated with the DSAA. You should not necessarily exclude a DSO on this basis; there are many DSOs who operate ethical companies, with their own internal code of standards and regulations who are not members of the DSAA.

Incentives

What incentives does the DSO provide their distributors? With these in mind you need to evaluate how difficult it would be to achieve the set targets. Most DSOs offer a range of incentives from small items like gift vouchers to the more lucrative, fully paid overseas trips with partners. It is important to consider the incentives offered by the DSO. Some distributors said they found the incentives helped motivate them to go that little step further. Incentives need not be just trips, and / or material possessions. Some of the distributors said they valued the opportunity they were given to meet celebrity presenters and knowledgeable experts. Many DSOs hold annual seminars and they invite some of the hottest and most well celebrated speakers to attend. Many distributors acknowledged this is an opportunity they ordinarily would not be afforded.

Compensation plan

The compensation plan offered by the DSO is extremely important in your assessment of which DSO you should join. It is difficult to state a definitive remuneration plan when there are many DSOs in the marketplace. Each will differ in how they reward and remunerate their distributors. Furthermore, some DSOs were naturally reluctant to provide the details of their compensation plan for the purpose of this book, as it is an integral part of their intellectual property and competitive advantage.

That being said, you should compare the percentage earned on sales. Most DSOs will pay 20 per cent commission on direct sales made by the distributor. Most DSOs pay their distributors within the month. Be very cautious of any DSO who offers you the opportunity to earn thousands. The reality is that if you could easily earn thousands, like that, in quick time or without much effort wouldn't we all be doing it? Don't be swayed by outrageous claims in the hope you will get rich quick.

You can maximise your earnings if you take the time to truly understand and appreciate the compensation plan offered. All legitimate and genuine compensation plans will provide distributors with an incredible opportunity to build a strong and viable business.

If you decide to build a team, the percentage you will receive on sales made by team members will greatly depend on where the distributor resides in the levels of your team. Make sure you understand exactly how the levels work and what level of compensation you can expect from various levels. Remember, once you start to create a team you are responsible for motivating and mentoring the team. You need to make sure the compensation is commensurate with your time and effort.

Spoilt for choice: How to pick the right Direct Selling Organisation.

117

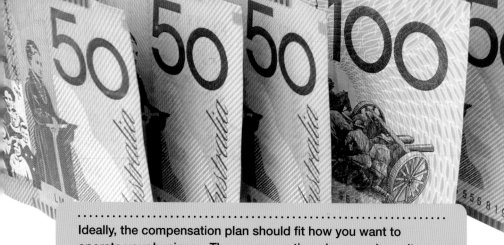

Ideally, the compensation plan should fit how you want to operate your business. The compensation plans can be quite comprehensive. They are designed to cater for all situations. It is a good idea to take the time to thoroughly understand the implications of the plan and what it could mean for you. Some cleverly created reward plans benefit the DSO more so than the distributor. For example, the compensation plan may state that a distributor is remunerated when they have reached a certain level of sales and receive no commission for sales made under this target. This means the DSO benefits from the sales made, however, the distributor completely misses out on a commission, even a pro rata commission, because they did not achieve the targets set by the DSO. Take care, it is extremely important to evaluate how and when you will be rewarded for your efforts.

One distributor explained, 'The compensation plan should be generous, offering a higher first-level commission'.

Most compensation plans are multi-level, meaning that distributors are remunerated according to what they do, rewards are scaled, and different rewards exist for varying activity, whereas the DSOs of door-to-door sales offer a flat rate, usually 20 per cent on sales made from the catalogues distributed.

Make sure you are able to sustain the proprietary rights of your position as you progress up the ladder. Life can throw a few curve balls from time to time, you wouldn't want to find you are relegated to a lower position for taking time off to have a baby for example. If the DSO has a car plan be sure that you understand the car program in detail before you agree to take on the car.

Sponsor

Most people are introduced to the opportunity to become a distributor; few simply call the company direct. It is extremely important to evaluate how you feel about the person presenting the opportunity. More than likely they will 'sponsor you in' and will become your upline mentor. If you like the idea of joining the industry but don't feel you necessarily have a rapport with the potential sponsor, don't feel compelled to sign up. Look around for another sponsor from the same DSO. The point here is that the sponsor plays a critical role – they will support, coach and mentor you so you are empowered to reach success. There is no point forcing a friendship if you feel it may be difficult to form a relationship with the sponsor. Seek someone else, as your success is dependent on it.

Spoilt for choice: How to pick the right Direct Selling Organisation.

Where to, once you have signed up to a

Direct Selling Organisation

Most people enter the direct selling industry through a sponsor. This is not mandatory, of course. It just so happens by way of the nature of the industry, people typically learn of the opportunity through a sponsor. In this chapter I will go through the process that generally applies once you have joined.

Training with your sponsor

To ensure the greatest opportunity for success, newly recruited distributors should seize every opportunity to undertake training. The successful distributors I spoke with attributed their success to their willingness to capitalise on every training opportunity they were offered.

Your sponsor will play an important role in your development and training plan. They will help guide, develop and train you to succeed. More importantly, they are there to lend a hand and support you when you come up against tough times. Rest assured your sponsor will hold your hand and walk you through the entire process. Your sponsor is responsible for

Where to, once you have signed up to a direct selling organisation.

121

Many of the distributors said they found the training sessions very valuable. Explaining, when they attended the training sessions they found they had an opportunity to connect with other distributors and discuss the challenges they were facing in their own business. Others noted the training sessions helped a great deal, providing an opportunity to learn from others – especially the more experienced and seasoned distributors.

teaching you the systems you will need to follow and implement in order to duplicate their success.

A word of caution, a distributor from a major nutritional supplement company explained to me during the initial sign up phase she warns her new recruits 'not' to talk to anyone about the opportunity. This may sound a little 'secret squirrel', however, there is logic in this approach. As the distributor explained to me ... new recruits are generally exploding with excitement to let friends and family know of the fantastic opportunity they have discovered. We all want to tell the world when we have discovered something amazing. She goes on to say that until the new recruit has

Your network marketing sponsor will help you to implement the systems required to structure your business, so that when you get busy, the business operates seamlessly. Distributors from all methods of direct selling agree that if you neglect to implement the right systems and structures, you can soon become swamped in paperwork.

Give It A Go!

undergone the necessary training, they are not in a position to properly convey the opportunity. It is important to be able to properly explain the opportunity otherwise sceptical family and friends will have greater justification for opposition to your new venture. When you first start out in direct selling it can be helpful to have the support of friends and family. If you know what to say and how to say it, chances are you will be in a better position to thoroughly explain the opportunity, and motivate your friends and family to support you rather than unintentionally turning them in the opposite direction.

The role of a distributor can be lonely from time to time. You will also find, like most things in life, you will have some terrific days where the orders are flooding in and conversely, you will have other days where you may face the cancellation of two consecutive parties. On the days when things have not gone quite as planned, many distributors said they found their training sessions very consoling. 'It is great to know you have the support of your colleagues, fellow distributors and associates in training', said one distributor. It is comforting to know you're not the only one to have had hosts cancel a presentation at the last minute.

Where to, once you have signed up to a direct selling organisation.

Team leaders regularly meet with their teams. One distributor said she prefers to meet with teams based on potential and willingness. There is little point in meeting a group of go-getters who are mixed with a number of individuals who see the opportunity more as a hobby. The team leader plays an important role in your relationship with the DSO and your success as a distributor. They are there to empower the members of their teams. They will provide the benefit of their experience and expertise to help team members succeed.

Training with your DSO

Once you have joined a DSO you will also be invited to participate in an in-depth induction and training program provided by the DSO themselves. It is highly recommended that you attend these sessions: seize every opportunity you can to develop and grow into the role of a successful distributor.

Most DSOs have 'distributor starter kits', which consist of basic manuals, brochures and DVDs. These kits are different to a sales kit, like the one used by a party plan distributor. Once you have signed up you will need to orient yourself with the contents of the kit and / or training material. Your sponsor will also provide training sessions to help orientate you through the kit and understand the training material provided.

Some sponsors I spoke with said they were happy to accompany their new recruits on their first few presentations.

The presentation process

The process of a presentation differs between network marketing and party plan, so we shall detail each process accordingly. It is worth noting that this is merely an outline – the actual DSO you join may undertake a similar process with minor variations. The process of any presentation is a procedure and consequently it is very important to attend training to not only understand the procedure but also be fluent enough in its successful application.

Network Marketing

Network marketing presentations are generally one-on-one. They can be physically face-to-face, or virtual, capitalising on the latest in technology. The first part of the meeting is spent getting to know the person. As one distributor explained … this is the time the distributor can quickly assess how they can be of benefit to this person. She indicated some new customers simply have a need for the product, whereas others may be seeking an entire 'sea change' such as a new and exciting business opportunity.

Once the distributor has an understanding of where and how they can help, they can begin to explain and discuss the benefits of the product they represent or opportunity on offer. Another distributor recommended that during the presentation, distributors should let go of their own agenda and concentrate on creating a rapport with the person.

The distributor may elect to cover the history of the DSO. They would then discuss the range of products on offer and how they relate to the prospect followed by a discussion on the different options available. These could include:

- Wholesale customer
- Business partner
- Retail customer

The distributor could then close with the question, 'Is there anything that interests you?'

In network marketing a different set of communication skills is required to successfully build your business. To become a successful network marketer you need to learn how to quickly identify the interests and needs of an individual prospect. Training with both your sponsor and DSO will help you to learn how to crystallise and understand the prospective customer's wants and needs. One distributor remarked to do well as a network marketer you must learn and develop good communication skills. You need to listen carefully to the answers provided by prospects, distinguishing between whether they are looking for a new business opportunity, a change in lifestyle or are they looking for solutions provided by the product.

Party Plan

Party plan is a little more involved. Overall, presentations can take up to 3 hours. The presentation is usually held in the home of the host. The host is responsible for organising the attendees, food and drink. The distributor is required to physically set up a display in the host's home prior to the arrival of the guests. It is a good idea to greet the guests as they arrive, recommends one distributor, who prefers to hand out catalogues while she is greeting guests on their arrival. Once everyone has arrived the distributor will introduce him / herself and thank the host. They will also provide the agenda or format for the event, followed by a brief background on the DSO and the products. The guests are free to touch or try on the products while the distributor discusses the benefits of the products. Depending on the nature of the product being sold, some distributors may need one-on-one time with the guests in the bedroom if they were fitting bras, for example. Alternatively, if they were demonstrating the application of skin care products they may have every attendee experiencing the product on their own face. The distributors of a cookware company actually make a main meal and dessert while they demonstrate the benefits of the cookware. While the main course is cooking, they begin on their closing, during which they would cover the main topics – the incentives of hosting a party and the opportunity to have your own business.

The actual order taking is again dependent on the product. The distributor of a lingerie company said she finds the ideal time to take orders is when she is professionally fitting the attendees with the bra they favour. Whereas the distributor from the cookware company revealed that they take orders shortly after discussing the host incentives and sponsorship.

Door-to-door sales

Similar to party plan and network marketing, you are usually introduced to door-to-door sales through a distributor. Catalogues distributed by distributors offer the recipients the opportunity to come on board. This is generally the first point of contact and from here the new distributor signs up, which could involve the purchase of catalogues. They are also allocated a designated area and provided with the opportunity to take up training.

Addressing your initial fears and

Getting started

Fears can arise and impact on your potential to succeed as a distributor. Rest assured all of the successful distributors I spoke with all started with feelings of trepidation and apprehension, it is completely natural. Having said this, you do need to implement measures to manage your fears in order to seize the opportunity at hand. In this chapter I will explain how you can 'get the ball rolling' on your career as a distributor and overcome any initial fears and concerns.

F eelings of fear are completely natural; don't beat yourself up for feeling a wee bit anxious. Fears can even set in when you least expect it; some distributors said they only started to feel anxious on the dawning of their first presentation. For some distributors their enthusiasm has masked their natural fear of presentation until the time they are required to do so. The good news is that all of these feelings are completely normal and best of all these negative feelings can be managed and eventually overcome.

Fear based on misinterpretation

OK! You have been offered an opportunity to join a DSO and your immediate reaction is, 'I love the product, but I can't sell to save myself'. It is a common response, however, it is a reaction based on misinterpretation. Out of the many hundreds of distributors I spoke with, not one indicated they were in the business of 'selling'. When offered the opportunity to join a DSO, it is important to change your perception of the opportunity offered. In reality, the role of a distributor can be summarised as a bearer of opportunities, a company spokesperson, not a salesperson. Let's look at it this way: a distributor has a kit, catalogue or product range they demonstrate and explain the benefits of the range, and they offer the person or persons an opportunity to purchase. No one is making anyone buy anything. From the opportunity to join the industry to hosting a party, the role of the distributor is merely informing their audience of the opportunities and associated benefits. People get very caught up with the word 'selling' and envisage that they are required to apply the cheesy, hard-and-fast sales approach ... nothing could be further from the truth.

For those with partners, consider your own personal situation. I am sure there have been times when you would have liked something that is not quite within the budget, where you have had to persuade your partner of the benefits. Your approach is no different in direct selling. There is an objective – you would like your partner to want the item as much as you do and would like them to buy into your enthusiasm for the product. So what do you do? You explain the benefits; you detail what this product can do for your lives. Presenting is exactly the same. It involves explaining to an audience the benefits and opportunities offered by the DSO you represent. Don't let your passion for a product offered by a DSO go to waste. Use your love for the product and tell others.

Getting the ball rolling

The starting point for any new entrant is the training and induction program. Any worthy DSO will host an extensive induction and training program. Whilst it is not mandatory, it is strongly recommended that you attend this or at least undertake the training whether it is via an online download or DVD. The information you will gain from these sessions will provide you with the best foundation to start and build your business. A number of the directors of various DSOs indicated that those who exit the industry soon after entry generally have not undertaken the necessary induction and training. You can overcome your initial fears and build confidence, through proper training and development. So please help yourself and do the training.

Addressing your initial fears and getting started

Overcoming the first step

The next step is the biggest step of all – the 'first party' or 'first presentation'. This is a big step.

Party plan

In party plan the first presentation is the catalyst that ignites the momentum for future presentations. Many distributors acknowledged that they started by asking family, friends and work colleagues - some even hosted the party in their own home. It is not uncommon to hear new entrants protest, 'I could never ask my friends or family to host a party. I wouldn't feel comfortable selling to my family or friends'. I put this to the seasoned distributors interviewed for this book, to which they responded that it is not about 'selling' per se but rather they recommended a change of mind-set. Distributors, especially new entrants, should think in terms that they are providing their friends and family with a product that will be of benefit to them. One distributor commented, 'It is not so much twisting the arm of a friend or family member to do you a favour, it is more about understanding what you have to offer and communicating the benefits to them' - whats in it for them.

Many distributors indicated, 'It really comes back to the training. You must have a clear understanding of what's in it for your friends'. A distributor of a major cookware company said that instead of asking for a favour, you actually offer a reward. If the person is willing to host a party and invite their friends, they will be rewarded with free products. This type of offer is much more appealing than the plea, 'Can you do me a favour?' Get a solid understanding of the benefits for the hostess – 'why should they host a party'. Explain these benefits in terms that would appeal to a potential host.

The wording you use to invite friends, family or associates to host a party is very important. You need the potential host to understand and recognise that it is a service you are offering, not a sale. A distributor from a DSO that specialises in lingerie says that when she encounters reluctance to invite friends her response is: 'you don't feel happy to share the best bra with your friends? This is a great opportunity to have a wonderful bra professionally

fitted'. You can see yourself from the wording and approach taken by this distributor that she is not instigating a push-to-sell product, but rather communicating the opportunity.

From your first few presentation you will need to book future presentations to start the momentum. It is a good idea to ask friends and family to invite people they wouldn't normally invite to your first party as this will make it easier to book future presentations. One distributor recommended, 'Make friends as soon as the attendees arrive; be friendly and approachable'. If the attendees do not warm to you because you lack charisma, it will not only be difficult to sell products, it will be even harder to book future presentations from the current presentation. Booking future presentations is pivotal to the survival of most distributors – especially those operating under a traditional party plan arrangement. Getting the first eight bookings is critical to your success as a distributor. Once you have these you can start to gain leverage, creating a snowball effect.

Network marketing – the first step

In network marketing the approach is a little different. To limit the number of 'no's' and to overcome the fear of rejection one distributor indicated, 'I qualify people on the spot'. She went on to explain … I don't tell everyone I meet about my business. Unlike party plan, this distributor said she finds that because of the personal nature of network marketing, it is better to qualify a person's level of interest by asking poignant questions. If I feel they are not interested in the business opportunity I would perhaps consider discussing the products I have available instead.

Network marketing distributors said it was very important to listen for appropriate conversation cues, explaining that you can strike up a conversation with a potential customer merely by listening for when and if it is at all appropriate to present the opportunity you have to offer.

A successful network distributor characterised her method of growing her business as a series of conversations. Other distributors questioned the authenticity of a new entrant who is reluctant to ask their friends and family to participate in a presentation. If you are really proud of the product and company you have joined and wholeheartedly believe in the product, then the chances are that you will feel compelled to tell all your friends about this wonderful product and worthy business opportunity. It comes back to your passion and enthusiasm.

Nevertheless, if you are reluctant to ask your friends and family you will need to consider alternative opportunities where you could meet potential customers. Consider other affiliations such as those listed below:

- Partner's work colleagues
- Sporting associations and clubs of which you are a member
- School newsletters
- Other associations, such as toast masters
- Parenting groups
- School committees
- Community noticeboards
- Play groups
- Kindergarten groups
- Social clubs

It is important to plug yourself into your local community to expand your network of contacts. You will need to get to know people. You could even consider the people you have regular contact with such as your hairdresser, doctor, and so on.

A distributor from a lingerie company explained how she secured a presentation by simply picking up an item at the post office. The woman behind the desk made a comment about the size of the box she had just signed for. Utilising the opportunity, by the time she had left the post office, the distributor had organised a date for a presentation with the postal worker.

Dealing with rejection

If you enter the direct selling industry under the belief that you will never face rejection, it is time to take off your rose-coloured glasses and think again. You will face the 'no, not for me' response. You will certainly face your fair share of critics, however, this is part and parcel of the industry. You will need to toughen up, if you wish to succeed. Even if you owned your own business or operated a web-based business you could still experience rejection or negative feedback – I can attest to that.

It is important to understand that a 'no thank you' does not necessarily mean they are saying no to you personally. The person is simply saying no to the opportunity presented to them. Perhaps they have no desire to improve their skin, take better care of their health or wear beautiful make-up. It will seem foreign to you because you are so passionate about the product that you can't understand why everyone doesn't see things the same way. Don't waste your energy getting upset or discouraged – for all the no's you may receive you can be assured there will be many more yes's, provided you keep on track and maintain your resolve.

Another point of view explained by the distributors I spoke with was that a 'no' sometimes means 'not right now'. It was important to ascertain the reason 'why' the person said, 'No thanks'. A 'No, not right now', means the door is still open at another point in time. We all lead busy lives and as a distributor you need to recognise that it is difficult for some people to make time. Do not take it personally!

Give It A Go!

The key to booking presentations is being open to talk about what you do as often as you can and without preaching or making a hard sell.

Many distributors recommend that you should always be prepared to let people know about your business: one distributor explained to me that she never misses an opportunity to tell people about her business in general conversation. She says she always carries information with her including business cards, catalogues and literature that she can readily hand out.

The most effective way to grow your business is to talk about your business. Some distributors are even engaging modern technology such as e-marketing and Facebook for promotional purposes.

Addressing your initial fears and getting started

Your Success

Success in the direct selling industry can be dependent on initial successes. A distributor from a cosmetics-based company noted, 'People who do not gain quick initial success will leave the industry sooner than others'. She explained that your initial success is part of the psychological confidence you need to grow. If you intend to succeed in this industry, do all you can in your earlier stages to provide yourself with a solid foundation and the confidence to continue.

If at first you don't succeed

J ane, a consultant from a global nutritional vitamin company, had a diverse career background starting as a travel consultant, to recruitment and finally moving into property management before relocating to New Zealand.

A single mum, with a five-month-old daughter to care for, Jane says she had to return to the workforce for financial reasons. 'I worked as a telemarketer and ended up in call centre recruitment', recalls Jane. 'I was stressed, working very hard, I had little extra money and was desperately trying to successfully juggle motherhood with a career'. Jane says that after a number of years she found she was actively looking for a change. Whilst not sure what type of change Jane explains, 'I was sure I wanted more time to spend with my family'. Jane had remarried and had a second child.

When she came across the DSO which she has now represented for the past ten years, Jane acknowledges, 'Direct selling was the last thing I was looking for'. Jane had tried direct selling previously and had worked in the industry on and off for a number of years. She admits she never really got it off the ground partly because she did not take her role as a distributor seriously. In hindsight, Jane believes it comes down to joining the right DSO. She says she is better suited to the network marketing structure. Initially, Jane had joined a party plan DSO where she was required to make a high level of retail sales. Armed with a great deal of scepticism, Jane sat as an anonymous figure in the seminar organised by the DSO. 'Something about the distributor just clicked with me and I felt compelled to explore the opportunity further', says Jane.

At the time Jane joined this specific DSO she had only been in her hometown for a short period of time. 'I didn't know many people', says Jane. I followed the systems and training provided by the DSO. Jane started by writing a list of names. She decided to approach ten people from whom she signed up two and those two then signed up another two. Working as little as ten hours a week, Jane's business grew quickly. She acknowledges this was due to her acceptance of the systems she was required to follow. Jane explains that, 'some people will experience little success in the direct selling industry because they fail to follow the systems and procedures taught by the DSO. Instead, they treat the opportunity as a hobby'. She makes the important observation: 'Some people will see the role as a hobby as opposed to an opportunity where your income is dependent on performance'. Jane believes some individuals, left to their own devices, are less responsible and accountable. It was important for Jane to follow the methodologies of the DSO if she wanted to replicate the achievements of the successful distributors before her.

Whilst Jane's business grew quickly she was not without her critics. Jane's family was not impressed with her decision to enter the direct selling industry. Her husband was supportive but Jane later discovered that he was far from happy with her decision. Jane's direct family was less supportive and some of Jane's family members thought she would fail because she had not made a success of her previous association with the direct selling industry. They could not understand why she was willing to give away a secure full-time paying position. 'I decided not to force my direct selling business upon my family even though they were happy to use the products of the DSO!

Give It A Go!

Jane believed it would be better for all concerned if she did not harp on the wonderful opportunity at hand. Jane offers up this advice for those considering entering the industry. If you beleive your move into direct selling, could potentially ruffle a few family feathers then 'make sure your partner understands everything you are doing and how important it is to you'. Budding distributors need to understand their partner has a belief system too and they are entitled to their opinion, but continuing to butt heads is unproductive for both parties.

For those considering joining a DSO, Jane highly recommends you consider why you wish to join. Jane says attitude is a big determining factor in your success in the direct selling industry. 'I knew I wanted to change my lifestyle. I was motivated by these strong personal desires. I just wanted to be a mum', states Jane.

Jane says that in her experience some people are sold into a dream without really knowing what is required or why they have joined. She urges potential distributors to really look at what is required of them. Understand that you may need to grow as a person. Jane likens the role to that of a warrior with a strong character. A lot of people enter the industry and are not as strong on the inside and in their first instance of 'rejection' they crumble and cannot move forward. Jane reinforces that if you are willing and prepared to grow as a person, you will develop the strong and confident personality that will equip you to leap over upsets.

The benefits for Jane have been life changing. Jane admits she still has to make sacrifices to run her business, however, these are not sacrifices on important issues. 'I am able to drop off and pick up my children from school; I am able to exercise with my husband since he was able to retire from full-time work at the age of 41', says Jane.

Besides the financial benefits gained from her role as a distributor, Jane has grown as a person. She admits she is a better person today than she was ten years ago.

How you can
Grow your
Business

In the direct selling industry you can grow your business through several strategies. Depending on the DSO, you are not solely restricted to earning commissions from product sales. In this chapter I will detail the strategies you can employ to grow your business.

Build a team

DSOs, governed by a network marketing structure, rely on building teams and recruiting new people to the business. If you are gun-shy of group presentations, network marketing offers an excellent opportunity to utilise your leadership skills to develop a team to generate a residual income.

How you can grow your business.

DSOs who implement a hybrid structure allow their distributors to earn an income by either building teams, retailing the product, or both. Sponsoring other distributors into your team and leveraging from members within your team is a fantastic way to build your business without undertaking a great deal of additional work. 'Sponsoring' is a term used whereby you sign up a new distributor on behalf of the company. It does not mean you pay for their start-up kit. Distributors of the hybrid structure can decide to focus on building a team or retailing the product or both; it depends entirely on the provisions of the DSO. The distributor who creates the team, sponsoring in new distributors, will earn a commission from each sale made by a member of the team. The amount of the commission will naturally vary between DSOs.

A distributor from one DSO explained that she preferred to build teams of distributors, coaching the distributors she sponsors on how they can achieve even greater success. She retails some product in order to be compliant with the DSOs' regulations and guidelines. She went on to explain that when building her team she will use different angles of her own story depending on the market of women to whom she is presenting. 'If I am presenting the business opportunity to a group of young mums, I will relate my own story of how I was once an at-home mum who was dedicated to finding an alternative way to fund my child's private school education. Whereas, if I were speaking to an older mum I would explain how direct selling has provided me with a lifestyle; She recommends that distributors who are keen to grow through the creation of teams should articulate different sides of their own personal experience and use the one that would best resonate with the audience they wish to appeal to.

Give It A Go!

Add-on sales

Other distributors recognise the importance of 'value-added selling'. They recommend that if distributors are looking to grow their business in terms of retail sales dollars they should consider promoting products that complement each other, effectively selling two products instead of one. 'Offer suggestions and explain why', was the recommendation from one distributor. This way you won't feel like you are being pushy. It is a good idea to offer ideas they haven't yet considered, explaining how this would help them to use the product better. As one distributor commented, 'If you have been thorough and informed the customer of their options, chances are the customer will not return home having wished they had purchased an item but didn't because the benefits were not made clear to them. Remember – success in direct selling is dependent on providing good customer service. We all know the disappointment of arriving home with a brand new product to find it would have satisfied your needs far better if you had purchased the extra add-ons. It is important to attend the training so you can thoroughly understand the alternative and complementary products available to offer your customer.

How you can grow your business.

Relationships – stay in touch

Creating and maintaining long-lasting customer relationships through customer service is critical to your success in the direct selling industry. Many DSOs sell 'consumer' products that turn over, meaning the customer will eventually need to replenish their stock of product, so they will reorder through you. Creating and developing strong relationships with your customers will ensure they return time and time again. Repeat orders are an excellent way to build your business. Chances are the customer will not require another party and they will be comfortable reordering straight from your catalogue. Whilst little effort is required to earn the commissions on these sales, however, a greater effort is required to maintain the relationships you make with your customers. The key is to be proactive, stay in touch and maintain contact whether it is by phone or email. Just like the owner of a small business, you should be reminding your customers of your services at least every 3–6 months. This would ensure your business is at the forefront of their mind-set. It is a good idea to maintain accurate customer records so you can readily identify what the customer last ordered and when, and this way you will know when to call without appearing too pushy. Accurate customer records will also help you to ensure you don't leave it too long between purchases whereby you risk the customer switching brands.

Give It A Go!

Customer service

Providing a high level of customer service is quintessential to the growth of your business. Superior customer service, results in strong word of mouth referrals. Customers grateful for the experience you have provided them, will readily refer your business to their friends, family and colleagues. Positive word of mouth is unquestionably, advertising money can't buy. Grow your business by giving your customers a real reason to refer you.

If you are considering joining a door-to-door sales DSO, providing a high level of customer service is the best way to grow your business. When delivering the order, distributors have an optimal point in time to build a relationship with their customer. This includes being pleasantly dressed, appropriately groomed, and doing all of the little things that ultimately add up to a greater positive impression and stronger customer relationship.

A director of a new door-to-door sales DSO said many door-to-door distributors neglect to seize the after-sales opportunities that exist to build and grow a business. Post-sale, when you are delivering the customer's order is an excellent time to get to know your customer. He offered this advice to door-to-door distributors: 'Take the time to contact the customer after their purchase has been received and don't be afraid to ask how they enjoyed the product'.

How you can grow your business.

Why do
some people
Fail?

There is little dispute that the reputation of the direct selling industry has suffered in the past. It is worthy of discussion, in this chapter I will explain why the industry has attracted a negative reputation and how this has unfortunately contributed to why some people fail in direct selling. I hope at the conclusion of this chapter you too can see the real and viable opportunities offered by the direct selling industry.

D irect selling began in Australia in the early part of the 1900s. In the years following the Second World War direct selling began to attract Australian companies in increasing numbers. The industry began to really emerge in the early 1960s when the large American DSOs began to operate in Australia. At the same time there were a handful of unscrupulous business operators who saw the industry as an opportunity to make a 'quick buck'. There were infamous pyramid-selling organisations and schemes. These schemes promoted a range of various wealth building opportunities. They enticed distributors by making outlandish claims. They offered participants the opportunity to earn thousands of dollars for little work. Unfortunately, this was not the case and a number of individuals felt cheated. Whilst pyramid-selling is now illegal, the reputation of the industry was tarnished and similar to old fables, the stories of how individuals were 'cheated' has carried on through the generations to follow. These stories are rebirthed and embellished when distributors fail. They tell their friends, 'It didn't work for me' without explaining perhaps why it didn't work. There are several reasons why a distributor fails in direct selling.

Succumbing to a lack of support

One of the main reasons a distributor will fail to succeed in this industry is due to the lack of support they receive from their partner, family and / or friends. It is incredibly hard to go against the grain, facing ridicule and humiliation for the choices you have made. It is easier to give up rather than stand your ground. Some of the distributors I spoke to had to overcome the intense pressure and scrutiny of their partners, family and friends they all agreed that they had personally grown from the experience – many in fact citing that they are stronger and more confident people for it.

If you are facing a lack of support on the home front, don't give up and spend a life wondering 'what if', summon the courage to wade through, seek alternative sources of support such as fellow distributors or your team leader. Pick a role model or mentor who may have faced similar challenges and seek to model your own behaviour and mind-set.

Failure to seize the opportunity

If you don't seize the opportunity with both hands you will achieve mediocre results. If you want serious results, you must take your role as a distributor seriously. You cannot expect to succeed at anything you do in life with a ho-hum attitude. Take, for example, an Olympic athlete – they don't turn up to training every other day or when they feel like it. They are constantly training and competing. They set themselves realistic goals and targets. Your attitude to the role of a distributor is pivotal to your success. If you believe your effort and determination to succeed would be half-hearted, then you should not consider becoming a distributor. It is all or nothing. Similar to anything in life, you get out what you put in and there are no short cuts.

Distributors will fail if they don't make an effort to meet people and make bookings for presentations. Irrespective of whether you join party plan or network marketing, the success of your business is greatly dependent on meeting new people, telling them about the opportunity, hopefully leading to a presentation. Bookings are the lifeblood of distributors in the direct selling industry.

Similarly in door-to-door sales, if you don't regularly deliver catalogues you won't reap the rewards. You must do the activity in order to enjoy the success.

Lack of realistic goals

You need to set yourself realistic goals. Some of the distributors pointed out the reason why some distributors fail to succeed is because they don't set realistic goals – some don't even set themselves any goals! Setting realistic goals is an excellent way to empowre and motivate yourself to want to succeed. Once you become a distributor it is a good idea to contact your team leader and discuss, what you can realistically expect to achieve given a set time frame. You need the guidance of an experienced team leader to help you set the right goals and targets. One of the quickest ways to become disillusioned and risk going off-track is to set unrealistic goals. Similar to losing weight, if you are looking for big numbers it won't happen overnight. Nor is it healthy to expect to lose a significant amount of weight in a short period of time. Similarly, don't expect to earn large sums of money as soon as you sign up. You would have to work like crazy to make big numbers in a short period of time and this is certainly not good for your health. Unrealistic goals can work against you. A person who fails to achieve a desired weight loss is more likely to binge or fall off the wagon, so to speak. The same applies in the direct selling industry – when you fail to achieve a desired result you can become disheartened and risk losing your motivation to continue.

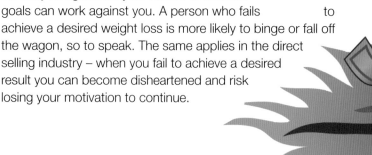

Believing it will all just happen

Unfortunately for some who join a DSO, there is a belief it will all just happen. They see the direct selling industry as a licence to print money. Some new recruits fail to realise they are solely responsible for ensuring their own success. Certainly many DSOs will provide the resources, infrastructure, systems, support, marketing, inspiration, motivation and everything else you could possibly need to make your business a success. However, what they cannot provide is the 'right attitude and actual action'. You need to muster the determination, desire and passion to want to succeed. Unfortunately, this is not a feeling you can readily purchase from the supermarket; it must come from within. For some distributors, the burning desire to succeed was a direct result of life-changing circumstances. Some distributors found themselves financially destitute after their partner had walked out and the basic human need to provide for their family propelled them to want to succeed. Others facing less dire straits acknowledged the desire to want to spend more time with their children; watching and guiding their development provided the quintessential fire in the belly to succeed as a distributor. One distributor explained her motivation was born from a case of guilt. She felt guilty because her partner had to go to work and missed out on seeing the children. She wanted to create an income stream that eased this pressure. To date, her husband has resigned from his career and now assists her in the business. It doesn't matter what your motivation is, whether it is simply to pay off the mortgage or have money for a holiday, the fact remains that without motivation you will inevitably fail. Identify your motivation – what is your 'why'? Why have you decided to join?

Now many will reply, 'to make a little extra money' and that's fine, but go further than this. Why do you want the extra money? Work this part out and you will have your motivation. If you intend taking a holiday at the end of the year get brochures, work out the costs, cut out pictures, stick them on your fridge and have a constant reminder of why you have joined the direct selling industry.

Struggling with rejection

All distributors will face the words 'no thank you' throughout their careers as a distributor. It is part of the role of being a distributor. How you deal and cope with the dismissal of your offer will greatly determine your success as a distributor. Distributors who do not cope well will certainly exit the industry relatively soon after signing on. If you are considering joining the direct selling industry or have just recently joined it, you need to train yourself to accept 'no thank you' and not take it personally. The person is not saying 'no' to you, they are saying 'no' to the opportunity and that is separate to you as a person. Some distributors will prematurely quit the industry because they have misread a person's response. When a person says 'no thank you', they could well mean, 'No, not just at the moment'. Alternatively, they may not have adequate information so they can fully appreciate why they should say 'yes' to the opportunity on offer. Part of your role as a distributor is reading between the lines and ascertaining whether the potential host is saying 'no' because they don't believe they need the benefits gained from hosting a presentation or benefits from the product or whether they are saying 'no' because the opportunity does not neatly fit in with their schedule at the moment.

Fear of asking for an opportunity to present

Some distributors acknowledged they have witnessed new entrants struggle to differentiate between the idea of offering an opportunity and feeling like they are being pushy, as if they were asking people to host a presentation in their honour. Successful distributors agree that the issue centres on the distributor's mind-set. It is important to always remember when asking someone to host a presentation or meet with you, focus less on you and more on what you have to offer and the benefits to be gained from hosting a presentation or catching up. It must be about them not you. Consider changing the terminology you use when booking your next presentation. One distributor recommended against saying, 'Could you host a presentation for me?' to 'I have discovered a great opportunity. Would you like to be … professionally fitted, or would you like a free cooking class?' The key is to emphasise the benefit for them, what will the host get out of having a party. Or why should the person meet with you to discuss the benefits and opportunities offered by your product?

It is important to understand you are offering an opportunity. You are not asking anyone to do anything for you. If you start believing that you are asking someone to host a presentation on your behalf, every 'no' you receive will more than likely feel like a personal rejection. If you find you are struggling with the idea of asking strangers to host a presentation, don't despair and give up! Take the time to identify and articulate the benefits a host would gain from hosting a presentation. Focus on these benefits and then script out how and what you could say to a potential

host. Scripting what you could say will help prepare you and ensure you market the opportunity as best you can. Focus on why the host should host a party or why the customer should meet with you.

Dismiss the systems

Distributors who refuse to follow the tried and tested systems developed and taught by the DSOs will more than likely exit the industry relatively quickly. While some DSOs will sell the same products, what they teach and how they instruct their distributors to succeed in the industry will always differ. Even if you have been in the industry with another DSO, you should still attend the training and induction programs facilitated by the DSO you have joined. As one distributor explained to me, she has watched distributors enter the industry who have enjoyed very distinguished careers. Some are less willing to learn new systems and procedures, and are stuck in their own way of doing things. If you are closed to learning new methods, techniques, systems and procedures, chances are you will not succeed in the direct selling industry. It is important to be open to change and as one distributor said, 'It is equivalent to unlearning all you have learnt and starting with a blank canvas'.

Understand the business ladder

Unfortunately, some distributors fail to understand the logic of the business ladder and are disheartened by the notion that 'only those at the top truly profit'. The rationale is that those at the top have had to work all the way up, too. You will always remain at the bottom of the ladder if you don't put in the time, effort and work required to climb the ladder. Sadly, some distributors will prematurely exit the industry before they have adequately given themselves an opportunity to get to the next step.

I am left with little doubt, after months of research, that there exists a real and viable opportunity to build a supplementary income and / or residual income through the direct selling industry.

However, having said this and before you sign up you need to really assess yourself and ask yourself whether you have what it takes. It is not about skills, or ability or even education. It is about attitude! Do you have the right attitude? Do you want to succeed, and if so why? Success in this industry is commensurate with a true understanding and appreciation of why you have decided to join the industry. Like most things in life, you may experience many wonderful and well-celebrated successes in your time in the direct selling industry and equally you will experience your share of challenges and difficult times. A clear understanding of why you have joined the industry will be critical during stressful times. Like a rudder on a boat, it will help to navigate you through and help you to weather stormy waters.

Similarly, you must temper your expectations; certainly you can expect to succeed with hard work, persistence and consistency. However, you cannot expect to 'make it' straight away. This is predominantly where many entrants into the industry fall down. They expect too much, too soon. I hope from your observations of my research that you can conclude that great success takes a while. You will be far better placed if you temper your expectations relative to your own level of effort and time in your role as a distributor.

Give it a go!... What have you got to lose?

Self-Assessment Exercises

To help you decide whether the direct selling industry is for you or not, I have devised a self-assessment section. The questions and answers should be used as a guide to help you to discover whether the role of a distributor is really for you.

Be sure to store your answers in a safe place. Should you decide to become a distributor, your answers could be a source of motivation when facing challenging times. Often when we confront challenges and hard times we can forget why we were motivated to act in the first place.

1. Write down why you want to become a distributor.

What are your top three motivators?

Motivation	Why does this motivate you to join the direct selling industry?

2. Are you ready to join the industry?

Circle the box with the answer that best describes you.

	1	2	3
Are you a 'go-getter'	Yes, if I see an opportunity I will seize upon it.	I need someone to motivate and encourage me.	I do things as and when I am up to them.
Are you focused and committed?	I am dedicated. I see things through to their completion. I am motivated by my goals and ambitions.	I try to finish what I start but sometimes put things on hold if I am interrupted.	I hardly ever finish the things I start. I get sidetracked very easily, especially if the going gets tough.
Do you have a strong desire for achievement?	Yes, I regularly set goals for myself.	Yes, but I am not sure what it is that I want to do.	No, I have no life goals. I would prefer to take each day as it comes.
Are you confident within yourself?	I have always felt assured within myself.	The level of my confidence will vary depending on the situation. My confidence tends to grow with experience.	I am not confident at all. It takes a lot of courage for me to put myself out there, outside my comfort zone.
Are you organised?	Yes, I often write 'to do' lists, I enjoy multi-tasking and making short-term and long-term plans.	I am partially organised though I do forget things on occasion. I need to learn to manage my time effectively.	I am constantly forgetting things. I regularly find myself in chaotic situations.

	1	**2**	**3**
Are you happy to assess your mistakes and learn from them?	I regularly assess the decisions I make. I learn from them and adapt my ways accordingly.	I don't regularly review my decisions unless mistakes are pointed out. I am happy to look into my mistakes once I have realised I have made them.	I never review my decisions. I feel that if things don't turn out as planned it was not my fault but more likely other factors unrelated to me.
Are you resourceful?	I am very self-sufficient at sourcing several solutions to address a specific problem. I like to think outside the square.	I am satisfied with the first viable answer to a problem. I don't usually look too far for an answer.	I don't enjoy searching for solutions. I believe the answer should come naturally.
Do you enjoy networking and meeting new people?	I can develop a good rapport with all types of personalities. I enjoy meeting people and get along with most people I meet.	I am a little shy. However, once I feel comfortable in my environment the shyness subsides and I usually fit right in.	I don't enjoy socialising and meeting new people. I have a certain group of friends and am more than happy to keep to the group.
Do you get frustrated when you encounter challenging times?	I take pleasure in finding ways to solve problems; I enjoy the search for solutions and feel enormous satisfaction when I have overcome a challenge.	I feel stressed when I am not sure how to get over an obstacle but still persist to find a solution.	I can become extremely disinterested when confronted with challenging obstacles.

	1	**2**	**3**
Do you let the opinions of others get to you?	I address the important things and pay less attention to the unimportant opinions. I see constructive criticism as a positive.	I am not easily offended. I get upset with the negative opinions of family and friends until I learn to deal with the critics.	I am extremely sensitive. I do not take criticism well at all. I value the opinions of family and friends more than my own.
Do you believe you can readily earn an income without hard work?	I believe you get what you put in. I don't believe in a free lunch and I am motivated to work towards a financial goal knowing I have the power to achieve what I desire.	I am inspired by the success of others. I am motivated to achieve and understand my efforts are a direct result of my application.	I think successful people are lucky people. They were in the right place at the right time.
Are you empathetic?	I feel for others. I can identify with and understand another person's circumstances even if I personally have not experienced it.	I often need to have experienced the same situation to feel a deeper sense of compassion, however, I can appreciate a person's misfortunes and circumstances.	I rarely feel empathyfor others. I try to distance myself from others so I don't take on another person's baggage.

If you have crossed mostly the answers in Column One – congratulations! The chances are that you would more than likely make an excellent distributor. You are up for the challenges faced by all distributors. Your tenacity and appreciation for hard work will set you on the right path towards success.

If you have ticked the majority of answers in Column Two – don't despair. This does not mean that you should not consider direct selling. Your answers simply indicate that for you, it is very important you choose a sponsor, mentor, or team leader who can help coach you through the hard times. With the right help and attitude you will succeed. But it is extremely important you attend training sessions and you seek out all the help you can to get yourself through. Remember, help is on hand for those who seek the answers they need!

Finally, if you have ticked the majority of answers from Column Three – I would strongly suggest you don't join the industry. Your success in direct selling is greatly dependent on yourself and without a strong desire to succeed you will struggle and more than likely give up. You need to be motivated and confident not only to meet people but also to seek the answers when facing tough times.

3. What are the pros and cons of joining the industry?

Pros	Cons

Now consider which side outweighs the other. Obviously, if your positives for joining the industry are favourable, you should consider 'giving it a go'.

However, if the negatives far outweigh the positives, there is little point forcing yourself to go into something you know from the start will be difficult. It is a lot like dieting or joining a gym to lose weight. You see the success you could achieve, you identify with the trim, taut model who has managed to achieve your ideal figure, and you know deep down that in order to achieve the success you will resent giving up the afternoon biscuit for a bowl of cabbage soup or stomping for five minutes on the monotonous treadmill. However, you figure miracles do happen and you sign up anyway. Chances are that because the negatives far outweighed the positives from the beginning, you won't succeed.

If you are going to join the industry you must be 100 per cent positive you will succeed or you will be doomed from the beginning.

4. Choosing a DSO to represent

The questions below require a 'yes' or 'no' answer. If you are able to confidently provide a 'yes' or 'no' answer it means you have given them adequate consideration. However, if you cannot confidently say 'yes' or 'no', chances are you have not done enough research into the DSO. Now is a good time to look a little further before you sign up.

1. Are you passionate about the DSOs product range?
2. Are you satisfied with the compensation plan? Does the reward balance out the work-load?
3. Is the product range capable of generating repeat sales?
4. Does the DSO have a favourable reputation in the industry?
5. Does the DSO utilise technology to enable you to sell more and are you comfortable with your role and responsibilities to the DSO?
6. Do you believe you will receive adequate training (both induction and ongoing) to support your role in the organisation?
7. Are there any restrictions that could limit or hinder your success?
8. Can you market your product range as you see fit?
9. Are they a member of the DSAA?
10. Are you motivated by the incentives offered by the DSO?

5. Prepare a plan

Use the following table to create a plan. Write down your goals, give an appropriate completion date and structure your date so you can achieve the target within the given time frame. It is also a good idea to measure your success once the date has passed by looking at how effectively you have achieved your goals.

Goal	Target date	Measure of success

Index

Index

Give It A Go!

Index

Give It A Go!

Index

Give It A Go!

THE END

www.giveitagowhathaveyougottolose.com.au